Justice in Motion: Exploring the Dynamics of Criminal Law

In a society governed by laws, criminal law stands as a pillar of justice, safeguarding the rights of individuals and maintaining social order. From ancient civilizations to modern democracies, criminal law has played a crucial role in shaping the contours of justice and holding individuals accountable for their actions. As the cornerstone of the legal system, it is a dynamic and ever-evolving field that reflects the changing values, societal norms, and challenges of each era.

"Justice in Motion: Exploring the Dynamics of Criminal Law" embarks on a compelling journey through the multifaceted world of criminal law, delving into its foundational principles, practices, and the intricate interplay between individuals, communities, and the legal system. This book aims to illuminate the complex dynamics at play within criminal law and foster a deeper understanding of its impact on societies worldwide.

In this comprehensive exploration, we will traverse the historical development of criminal law, unveiling its origins and evolution across different civilizations. From early codes of Hammurabi to the principles of English common law and the modern statutory frameworks, we will witness how criminal law has evolved to adapt to changing societal needs while upholding the ideals of justice and fairness.

Furthermore, "Justice in Motion" will delve into the fundamental principles that underpin criminal law, such as the presumption of innocence, the burden of proof, and the role of intent in determining guilt. We will uncover the delicate balance between protecting individual liberties and ensuring public safety, as well as the challenges of addressing emerging crimes facilitated by advancements in technology.

Throughout the book, we will explore various aspects of criminal law, including the process of investigation, arrest, and trial, as well as the role of legal professionals, law enforcement agencies, and the judiciary. Drawing from real-life case studies and legal precedents, we will analyze how criminal law adapts to novel situations and sets legal standards to guide future cases.

Beyond the confines of the courtroom, "Justice in Motion" will examine the broader implications of criminal law on societal attitudes, community relations, and the pursuit of a more just and equitable world. We will explore the role of restorative justice, rehabilitation, and alternative dispute resolution in shaping a criminal justice system that seeks to heal wounds and reintegrate offenders into society.

Lastly, this book aims to stimulate critical discussions on the challenges faced by modern criminal justice systems, from addressing systemic biases and ensuring access to legal representation to promoting evidence-based policymaking and balancing punitive measures with effective rehabilitation.

In this exploration of criminal law, "Justice in Motion" seeks to offer readers a comprehensive and thought-provoking analysis of the legal principles, social contexts, and human stories that shape the pursuit of justice in our ever-changing world. As we embark on this journey, we invite readers to examine the dynamics of criminal law and engage in meaningful dialogues on how we can foster a more just and compassionate society through the pursuit of justice.

I. Introduction

- The importance of criminal law in society
- Overview of the book's objectives and scope

II. Historical Development of Criminal Law

- Early systems of justice and retribution
- Ancient legal codes and their influence
- Development of criminal law in common law systems
- Emergence of modern criminal law principles

III. Foundational Principles of Criminal Law

- Presumption of innocence and burden of proof
- Elements of a crime: actus reus and mens rea
- The principle of legality and retroactive laws
- The concept of proportionality in sentencing

IV. Criminal Law in Practice

- The role of law enforcement in crime prevention and investigation
- Arrest, detention, and Miranda rights
- Criminal trials and the adversarial process
- The role of legal professionals: judges, prosecutors, and defense attorneys

V. Criminal Offenses and their Classifications

- Overview of different types of criminal offenses (e.g., violent crimes, property crimes, white-collar crimes)
- Felonies, misdemeanors, and their consequences
- Emerging crimes in the digital age (e.g., cybercrime, identity theft)

VI. The Evolution of Punishment and Correctional Systems

- Historical approaches to punishment and retribution

- Modern theories of punishment: retribution, deterrence, rehabilitation, and incapacitation
- The role of restorative justice and its impact on criminal sentencing

VII. Challenges in the Criminal Justice System

- Addressing systemic biases and promoting equal treatment
- Ensuring access to legal representation and legal aid
- Overcoming obstacles in the investigation and prosecution of crimes
- The impact of wrongful convictions and exonerations

VIII. Technological Advancements and Criminal Law

- Digital evidence and challenges in preserving its integrity
- The use of technology in crime detection and prevention
- Balancing privacy rights and law enforcement in the digital age

IX. Alternatives to Traditional Criminal Justice

- Diversion programs and community-based sentencing
- Problem-solving courts (e.g., drug courts, mental health courts)
- The role of restorative justice in resolving conflicts

X. Criminal Law and Human Rights

- Protecting individual rights in criminal proceedings

- The prohibition of torture and cruel, inhuman, or degrading treatment
- The right to a fair trial and due process

XI. Global Perspectives on Criminal Law

- Comparative analysis of criminal justice systems in different countries
- International criminal law and efforts to address transnational crimes
- Challenges in extradition and international cooperation in criminal matters

XII. Future Trends in Criminal Law

- The impact of emerging technologies on crime and law enforcement
- The role of artificial intelligence in criminal justice systems
- Innovations in criminal law and policy-making

XIII. Conclusion

- Recapitulation of key insights and themes discussed in the book
- A call to action for promoting a more just and effective criminal justice system
- The importance of ongoing dialogue and research in shaping the future of criminal law.

The importance of criminal law in society

Criminal law plays a pivotal role in society, serving as a vital framework for maintaining order, protecting individual rights, and upholding the values of justice and fairness. Its importance stems from several key factors:

1. Ensuring Public Safety: Criminal law defines and prohibits actions that are harmful to individuals and society at large. By identifying and punishing criminal behavior, it acts as a deterrent and promotes public safety, instilling confidence in citizens that their well-being is protected.

2. Upholding the Rule of Law: Criminal law embodies the principle of the rule of law, which ensures that all individuals, regardless of their social status or position, are subject to the same set of laws and are accountable for their actions. This principle fosters a sense of equality and promotes trust in the legal system.

3. Protecting Individual Rights: Criminal law safeguards the fundamental rights and liberties of individuals by setting boundaries on government power and protecting citizens from arbitrary arrest and punishment. It provides a mechanism for individuals to seek redress if their rights are violated.

4. Encouraging Respect for Others: Criminal law establishes societal norms and expectations, promoting respect for the rights and well-being of others. It helps maintain social cohesion by setting standards of conduct that reflect shared values.

5. Providing a Mechanism for Dispute Resolution: Criminal law provides a formal and structured process for addressing conflicts and disputes. Through criminal trials and sentencing, it offers a fair and impartial mechanism for resolving disputes and holding wrongdoers accountable.

6. Promoting Rehabilitation and Reintegration: Criminal law acknowledges the potential for rehabilitation and the reintegration of offenders into society. By providing sentencing options that focus on reform rather than solely punishment, it aims to reduce recidivism and create safer communities.

7. Protecting Vulnerable Populations: Criminal law recognizes the need to protect vulnerable populations, such as children, the elderly, and marginalized communities, from exploitation and harm.

8. Upholding Public Trust in Institutions: A robust criminal justice system that operates transparently and fairly fosters trust in government institutions and reinforces citizens' confidence in the rule of law.

9. Deterring Criminal Conduct: The threat of criminal punishment acts as a deterrent to potential offenders, discouraging criminal behavior and contributing to the prevention of crime.

10. Reflecting Societal Values: Criminal law evolves in response to societal changes and evolving values, reflecting the collective understanding of right and wrong in a given community or culture.

In summary, criminal law's significance lies in its ability to protect individual rights, maintain social order, and promote justice and accountability. It serves as a cornerstone of democratic societies, ensuring that laws are enforced fairly and equitably and that individuals are held responsible for their actions, thereby contributing to the overall well-being and stability of society.

Overview of the book's objectives and scope

"Justice in Motion: Exploring the Dynamics of Criminal Law" seeks to provide a comprehensive and insightful exploration of criminal law, its foundational principles, practices, and its profound impact on societies in the modern era. The book aims to offer a multifaceted perspective on criminal law, delving into its historical development, theoretical underpinnings, and real-world application within the context of contemporary democratic societies.

Objectives:

1. Comprehensive Understanding: The primary objective of the book is to offer readers a comprehensive understanding of criminal law, encompassing its historical evolution, theoretical foundations, and practical application in addressing criminal conduct.

2. Legal Principles and Practices: The book aims to elucidate the foundational principles of criminal law, such as the presumption of innocence, the burden of proof, elements of a crime, and the concept of proportionality in sentencing. Additionally, it explores the practical aspects of criminal law, including arrest procedures, legal representation, and the trial process.

3. Analyzing Challenges: "Justice in Motion" endeavors to analyze the challenges faced by modern criminal justice systems, including issues of systemic bias, access to justice, wrongful convictions, and advancements in technology.

4. Global Perspectives: The book provides global perspectives on criminal law, examining the

similarities and differences among criminal justice systems in various countries, as well as the role of international criminal law in addressing transnational crimes.

5. Emerging Trends and Innovations: It explores emerging trends and innovations in criminal law, including the impact of technology, artificial intelligence, and alternative approaches to punishment and correctional systems.

6. Social Justice and Human Rights: The book highlights the role of criminal law in promoting social justice, protecting human rights, and addressing the rights of vulnerable populations within the criminal justice system.

Scope:

1. Historical Context: The book delves into the historical development of criminal law, tracing its origins from ancient legal systems to its evolution in common law and statutory frameworks.

2. Legal Principles and Practice: It provides a comprehensive examination of the core principles of criminal law, including those governing the determination of guilt, sentencing, and the roles of various legal actors.

3. Criminal Offenses and Classifications: "Justice in Motion" covers an array of criminal offenses and their classifications, exploring crimes against persons, property, and society, as well as emerging crimes in the digital age.

4. Rehabilitation and Alternatives: The book discusses modern theories of punishment and explores the role of restorative justice and rehabilitation as alternatives to traditional punitive approaches.

5. Global and Comparative Perspectives: It incorporates

    global perspectives on criminal law, examining how different countries address crime and the complexities of international cooperation in criminal matters.

6. Technological Advancements: The book addresses the impact of technological advancements on criminal law, including challenges in preserving digital evidence and the use of technology in crime detection.

7. Human Rights and Social Justice: It explores the intersection of criminal law with human rights, addressing issues of due process, fair trial, and the protection of individual rights within the criminal justice system.

Overall, "Justice in Motion" aims to present a comprehensive and thought-provoking analysis of criminal law, its role in promoting justice, safeguarding rights, and addressing the challenges of the modern world. By encompassing a diverse range of topics, the book seeks to foster a deeper understanding of criminal law's complexities and its potential to shape a fairer and more just society.

Historical Development of Criminal Law

The historical development of criminal law can be traced back to ancient civilizations, where societies sought to maintain order and impose sanctions for harmful actions. Over the centuries, criminal law has evolved significantly, influenced by diverse cultural, religious, and legal traditions. Here is an overview of the key stages in the historical development of criminal law:

1. Ancient Legal Codes: The origins of criminal law can be found in ancient legal codes dating back thousands of years. One of the earliest examples is the Code of Hammurabi, developed in ancient Mesopotamia around 1754 BCE. This code prescribed specific punishments for various crimes and established the principle of "lex talionis" or "an eye for an eye."

2. Ancient Greece and Rome: Ancient Greek and Roman civilizations further contributed to the development of criminal law. In Athens, the legal system relied on a jury of citizens to determine guilt or innocence. Roman law, particularly under the Twelve Tables, established a set of written laws that applied to both civil and criminal matters.

3. Middle Ages: During the Middle Ages, criminal law was heavily influenced by religious norms and practices. Trials by ordeal and the concept of divine intervention in determining guilt or innocence were common. This period also witnessed the emergence of "common law" principles in England, which formed the basis for many modern legal systems.

4. Renaissance and Enlightenment: The Renaissance and

Enlightenment periods saw a shift towards more rational and humanistic legal systems. Legal scholars like Cesare Beccaria and Jeremy Bentham advocated for the reform of criminal laws, emphasizing the importance of proportionality in punishment and the need to deter crime through rational means.

5. Emergence of Modern Criminal Codes: In the 19th and 20th centuries, many countries codified their criminal laws, compiling them into comprehensive legal codes. These modern criminal codes aimed to unify and clarify criminal offenses and penalties.

6. International Criminal Law: The 20th century also witnessed the development of international criminal law, particularly after the atrocities of World War II. The Nuremberg and Tokyo Trials established the principles of prosecuting individuals for crimes against humanity, war crimes, and genocide.

7. Contemporary Developments: In modern times, criminal law has continued to evolve, adapting to social and technological changes. The recognition of human rights, due process protections, and the establishment of criminal justice systems with independent judiciaries have become hallmarks of modern criminal law.

Throughout history, criminal law has played a crucial role in shaping societies, promoting order, and protecting individual rights. Its evolution reflects the changing values and norms of each era, as well as the ongoing pursuit of justice and fairness in the face of new challenges and advancements. The historical development of criminal law serves as a foundation for contemporary legal systems and continues to influence the shaping of criminal justice policies and practices worldwide.

Early systems of justice and retribution

Early systems of justice and retribution were rudimentary forms of legal systems developed by ancient civilizations to maintain order and resolve disputes within their societies. These early systems varied greatly across different cultures and time periods, but they shared the common goal of addressing conflicts and seeking some form of retribution or resolution. Here are some examples of early systems of justice and retribution:

1. Blood Feuds: In tribal societies and early civilizations, disputes between individuals or families often resulted in blood feuds. When one person harmed or killed another, the victim's family sought revenge by inflicting harm on the offender or their family members. Blood feuds were deeply rooted in notions of honor, and they often perpetuated cycles of violence and vendettas.

2. Trial by Ordeal: In some ancient societies, trial by ordeal was used to determine guilt or innocence. This involved subjecting the accused to a painful or dangerous test, such as holding a red-hot iron or submerging the accused in water. The belief was that divine intervention would protect the innocent, and the guilty would suffer harm.

3. Trial by Combat: Trial by combat was another form of ancient justice, particularly in medieval Europe. In this system, the accused and the accuser would engage in physical combat, with the belief that the victor was favored by God and thus considered innocent.

4. Retaliation and Restitution: Many early legal systems focused on restitution rather than punishment. Offenders were required to compensate their victims or their families as a means of restoring the balance of justice. The severity of restitution often depended on the gravity of the offense.

5. Customary Laws: In tribal and pre-state societies, customary laws emerged to regulate behavior within the community. These laws were passed down through oral tradition and were enforced by community elders or tribal leaders.

6. Code of Hammurabi: The Code of Hammurabi, developed in ancient Mesopotamia around 1754 BCE, is one of the earliest recorded legal codes. It prescribed specific punishments for various crimes and established principles of "an eye for an eye" and proportionality in punishment.

7. Roman Law: The Roman legal system, particularly under the Twelve Tables, provided a more structured and codified approach to justice. It established written laws that applied to both civil and criminal matters and provided guidelines for resolving disputes.

8. Mosaic Law: The ancient Hebrew legal system, as laid out in the Mosaic Law, included principles of justice, restitution, and punishment. The Ten Commandments and other laws provided a moral and legal framework for the ancient Hebrew society.

These early systems of justice and retribution were influenced by the cultural, religious, and social norms of their time. While they lacked the complexity and formal institutions of modern legal systems, they played a crucial role in establishing social order and resolving conflicts within early civilizations. Over time, these early systems evolved and laid the foundation for the development of more sophisticated and structured legal frameworks in the subsequent centuries.

Ancient legal codes and their influence

Ancient legal codes were early written collections of laws and regulations that played a significant role in shaping legal systems and influencing subsequent legal developments. These codes emerged in various ancient civilizations and had a profound impact on the development of law and justice. Some of the most influential ancient legal codes include:

1. Code of Hammurabi (Babylon, Mesopotamia, c. 1754 BCE): The Code of Hammurabi, named after the Babylonian king Hammurabi, is one of the oldest and most well-known legal codes in history. Engraved on a stele, it consisted of 282 laws that governed various aspects of life, including family, property, trade, and criminal justice. The code is famous for its principle of "an eye for an eye, a tooth for a tooth," which sought to establish proportionality in punishment. The Code of Hammurabi heavily influenced subsequent legal systems and laid the groundwork for future codifications of law.

2. Laws of Eshnunna (Mesopotamia, c. 1930 BCE): The Laws of Eshnunna were another early legal code from Mesopotamia. It covered a range of legal matters, including family law, property disputes, and contracts. While less extensive than the Code of Hammurabi, the Laws of Eshnunna provided valuable insights into the legal practices of ancient Mesopotamia.

3. Hittite Laws (Hittite Empire, c. 1650-1200 BCE): The Hittite Laws were a collection of legal provisions from the Hittite Empire, an ancient civilization in Anatolia

(modern-day Turkey). These laws dealt with issues such as property rights, marriage, and contracts, providing a glimpse into the legal norms of the time.

4. Laws of Ur-Nammu (Sumer, c. 2100 BCE): The Laws of Ur-Nammu are one of the earliest known legal codes and were established by Ur-Nammu, a Sumerian king. While only fragments of this code have been discovered, it is considered an important precursor to later legal developments.

The influence of these ancient legal codes extended beyond the civilizations in which they originated. As writing and trade spread, knowledge of these laws reached neighboring regions, influencing the development of legal systems in adjacent cultures. The principles of justice, fairness, and proportionality embedded in these codes laid the foundation for the concept of the rule of law, which remains a fundamental principle in modern legal systems.

Moreover, the codification of laws in ancient times marked a significant advancement in legal thinking and practice. By providing written laws, these codes promoted transparency, consistency, and predictability in the administration of justice. They also underscored the idea that laws should apply equally to all members of society, regardless of their social status or background—a concept that remains central to modern legal systems.

The legacy of these ancient legal codes is evident in contemporary legal systems, where the principles they established continue to shape the foundations of justice and the rule of law. Their enduring influence highlights the enduring importance of written laws and the pursuit of fairness and justice in human societies throughout history.

Development of criminal law in common law systems

The development of criminal law in common law systems has been a gradual and evolutionary process, shaped by historical, cultural, and legal factors. Common law systems originated in England and were subsequently adopted and adapted by many countries, including the United States and other Commonwealth nations. Here are the key stages in the development of criminal law in common law systems:

1. Early Customary Law: Prior to the formalization of common law, English communities relied on customary law and unwritten traditions to address criminal conduct. Local customs and norms determined what acts were considered criminal and the corresponding punishments.

2. Emergence of Common Law Courts: During the Middle Ages, common law courts started to develop as a distinct legal system separate from ecclesiastical and royal courts. These courts, presided over by judges, gradually established a body of precedent and case law that would become foundational for the development of criminal law.

3. The Influence of Royal Courts: In the 12th and 13th centuries, royal courts began to assert their authority in criminal matters, leading to the centralization of criminal jurisdiction. This shift provided a more consistent approach to criminal law enforcement throughout England.

4. Writs and Pleas of the Crown: During the reign of King Edward I, writs and pleas of the crown were introduced to address offenses considered against the king's interests. This marked a significant step in the development of criminal law as it formalized the process for bringing criminal cases before the royal courts.

5. The Development of Criminal Law Precedents: As common law courts heard and decided cases, they began to create legal precedents that future courts would use as authoritative guidance in similar cases. These precedents established legal principles and interpretations that shaped the development of criminal law.

6. The Role of Statutes: While common law courts relied on precedent, the English Parliament also played a crucial role in the development of criminal law through the enactment of statutes. Statutes clarified and supplemented common law principles, addressing specific criminal offenses and prescribing penalties.

7. Blackstone's Commentaries: In the 18th century, Sir William Blackstone's "Commentaries on the Laws of England" became a seminal work in legal education and played a significant role in the codification of English common law principles. His writings helped systematize and explain criminal law concepts.

8. Codification and Modernization: Over time, common law principles were codified into formal statutory laws, providing greater clarity and accessibility to the legal system. These codifications, together with ongoing court decisions, contributed to the modernization and development of criminal law in common law jurisdictions.

9. Expansion of Common Law Jurisdictions: As British colonies and territories were established, they adopted English common law as the basis for their legal

systems. Over the centuries, common law principles evolved and were adapted to local circumstances, resulting in the diverse range of common law systems seen today.

Today, common law systems continue to develop and adapt to changing societal needs and values. The principles of stare decisis (following precedent) and the gradual evolution of legal doctrine remain essential aspects of common law systems worldwide, shaping the ongoing development of criminal law in these jurisdictions.

Emergence of modern criminal law principles

The emergence of modern criminal law principles can be traced to the historical development of legal systems and the evolution of societal norms. Several key factors contributed to the establishment of these principles, which form the foundation of criminal law in contemporary legal systems. Some of the most significant factors include:

1. Rule of Law: The concept of the rule of law, emphasizing that all individuals are subject to the same laws and no one is above the law, became a cornerstone of modern legal systems. This principle promotes the idea that the law is predictable, consistent, and applicable to everyone, including those in positions of power.

2. Codification of Laws: The codification of laws, organizing legal rules into comprehensive and written statutes, contributed to the modernization of criminal law. Codification increased legal certainty and accessibility, ensuring that criminal offenses and penalties were clear and transparent.

3. Due Process and Fair Trial: The notion of due process, which guarantees fair and impartial treatment to individuals accused of crimes, emerged as a fundamental principle. Fair trial rights, such as the right to legal representation, the presumption of innocence, the right to remain silent, and the right to confront witnesses, became essential components of modern criminal law.

4. Mens Rea and Actus Reus: The distinction between

mens rea (the mental state of the offender) and actus reus (the physical act or conduct) became integral to modern criminal law. The principle of requiring both elements to be proven ensures that criminal liability is based on intention and voluntary action.

5. Proportionality in Punishment: The principle of proportionality in sentencing, which seeks to match the severity of punishment with the seriousness of the crime, gained prominence. Modern criminal law aims to avoid excessive or overly lenient penalties and considers factors such as the gravity of the offense, the harm caused, and the offender's culpability.

6. Criminal Intent and Strict Liability: Modern criminal law distinguishes between crimes that require criminal intent (mens rea) and those that impose strict liability, holding offenders responsible for certain offenses even without proving intent. This differentiation ensures that those who knowingly commit wrongful acts face appropriate consequences.

7. Gradation of Offenses: Modern criminal law often classifies offenses into different categories, such as misdemeanors and felonies, based on their seriousness. This gradation allows for a more nuanced approach to sentencing and punishment.

8. Victim's Rights and Restorative Justice: The recognition of victim's rights and the promotion of restorative justice principles aim to provide support to victims of crime and facilitate healing and reconciliation between victims and offenders.

9. Human Rights and International Law: The development of modern human rights norms and international criminal law has influenced domestic criminal law principles. International conventions and treaties have established universal standards for addressing serious crimes, such as genocide, war crimes, and crimes against humanity.

These modern criminal law principles reflect society's evolving understanding of justice, fairness, and the protection of individual rights. As legal systems continue to develop and adapt, these principles remain central to the pursuit of justice and the maintenance of social order in contemporary societies.

Foundational Principles of Criminal Law

The foundational principles of criminal law serve as the bedrock of the legal framework in addressing criminal conduct and administering justice. These principles underpin the fair and effective operation of criminal justice systems worldwide. Here are the key foundational principles of criminal law:

1. Legality Principle: Also known as the principle of legality or nullum crimen sine lege (no crime without law), this principle dictates that an act can only be considered a crime if it is explicitly defined as such by law. The law must be clear, specific, and publicly accessible, providing fair notice to individuals about prohibited conduct and potential consequences.

2. Presumption of Innocence: The presumption of innocence holds that an accused person is considered innocent until proven guilty beyond a reasonable doubt in a court of law. This principle places the burden of proof on the prosecution to establish the guilt of the accused through credible evidence.

3. Actus Reus and Mens Rea: Actus reus refers to the physical act or conduct that constitutes a criminal offense, while mens rea pertains to the mental state or criminal intent of the offender. Both elements must generally be present for an act to be considered a crime, ensuring that criminal liability is based on a combination of voluntary action and culpable mental state.

4. Causation: Criminal liability requires a causal link between the act committed (actus reus) and the harm

caused or consequences resulting from the act. This principle ensures that individuals are held responsible only for the harm directly caused by their actions.

5. Proportionality: The principle of proportionality in punishment demands that the severity of the punishment be commensurate with the seriousness of the crime committed. This ensures that punishments are not unduly harsh or excessively lenient, promoting fairness in sentencing.

6. Double Jeopardy: The principle of double jeopardy prohibits a person from being tried or punished more than once for the same offense. This protection prevents individuals from being subjected to multiple prosecutions for the same alleged criminal conduct.

7. Right to a Fair Trial: The right to a fair trial guarantees that individuals accused of crimes have the right to a fair and impartial hearing before an independent and competent tribunal. It includes rights such as legal representation, the right to present evidence and witnesses, and the right to cross-examine witnesses.

8. Ex Post Facto Laws: Ex post facto laws are laws that retroactively criminalize conduct that was legal when committed. The principle prohibits the enactment of such laws, safeguarding individuals from being punished for actions that were not prohibited at the time they occurred.

9. No Punishment without Law: This principle, also known as nulla poena sine lege (no punishment without law), stipulates that individuals can only be punished based on pre-existing legal provisions. It reinforces the importance of adhering to the legality principle and ensures that penalties are not imposed arbitrarily.

These foundational principles are fundamental to the functioning of criminal justice systems, safeguarding individual rights, promoting fairness, and upholding the rule of law. They form the basis for legal procedures, trial processes, and the determination of criminal liability, aiming to strike a balance between the protection of society and the protection of individual liberties.

Presumption of innocence and burden of proof

The presumption of innocence and burden of proof are fundamental principles in criminal law that ensure a fair and just legal process for individuals accused of committing crimes. These principles serve as essential safeguards to protect the rights and liberties of individuals facing criminal charges. Let's explore each principle in detail:

1. Presumption of Innocence: The presumption of innocence, often expressed as "innocent until proven guilty," is a cornerstone of criminal law in most democratic societies. It asserts that an accused person is considered innocent of the alleged crime until the prosecution can prove their guilt beyond a reasonable doubt in a court of law.

The presumption of innocence serves several crucial functions:

- Protects Individual Rights: It upholds the fundamental principle that individuals should not be treated as criminals or punished before their guilt is established through a fair and impartial legal process.
- Shifts the Burden of Proof: The presumption of innocence places the burden of proving guilt squarely on the prosecution. It is not the responsibility of the accused to prove their innocence; instead, the prosecution must present sufficient evidence to convince the court of the accused's guilt.
- Prevents Arbitrary Detention: The presumption of innocence helps prevent arbitrary arrests and detention. It requires authorities to provide credible

evidence of guilt before depriving individuals of their freedom.

- Preserves the Dignity of the Accused: Recognizing individuals as innocent until proven guilty respects their human dignity and protects them from social stigma and harm that may result from unfounded allegations.

2. Burden of Proof: The burden of proof refers to the responsibility of the prosecution to present evidence and establish the guilt of the accused beyond a reasonable doubt. It is the prosecution's duty to convince the judge or jury that the accused committed the alleged crime.

The burden of proof serves the following purposes:

- Ensures Fairness: Placing the burden on the prosecution ensures that the state has a substantial obligation to support its claims against the accused. This helps ensure a fair and balanced legal process.
- Encourages Precision in Legal Arguments: The prosecution must present clear and compelling evidence to meet the burden of proof. This requirement encourages thorough investigation and rigorous legal arguments, promoting the reliability of the justice system.
- Protects against Convicting the Innocent: Requiring a high standard of proof (beyond a reasonable doubt) minimizes the risk of convicting innocent individuals. It is designed to prevent wrongful convictions and miscarriages of justice.
- Safeguards Against Abuses of Power: Placing the burden of proof on the prosecution acts as a safeguard against the misuse of governmental power in criminal proceedings.

In summary, the presumption of innocence and burden of proof are interconnected principles that work together to ensure a fair trial and protect the rights of the accused in criminal proceedings. The presumption of innocence establishes the baseline status of innocence for the accused, while the burden of proof places the onus on the prosecution to present compelling evidence of guilt before a conviction can occur.

Elements of a crime: actus reus and mens rea

The two essential elements of a crime are actus reus and mens rea. These Latin terms represent the physical act and the mental state of the offender, respectively. Both elements must generally be present to establish criminal liability. Let's explore each element in detail:

1. Actus Reus (Guilty Act): Actus reus refers to the physical act or conduct that constitutes a criminal offense. It is the external behavior or action committed by the accused that is prohibited by law. Actus reus can take various forms, such as:

   - Voluntary Actions: The act must be a voluntary and conscious choice by the individual. Accidental actions or involuntary behavior typically do not fulfill the actus reus requirement.

   - Omissions: In some cases, a failure to act (omission) can also constitute actus reus if there was a legal duty to act and the individual willfully neglected that duty. For example, failing to render aid to a person in distress when there is a legal obligation to do so may be considered criminal.

   - Possession: Possessing illegal substances or stolen property with the knowledge of their nature and control over them can fulfill the actus reus requirement in certain offenses.

To establish actus reus, the prosecution must demonstrate that the accused engaged in the physical act described by the criminal statute. Merely having a criminal intention or desire to commit a crime is not sufficient; the actual act or conduct must be present.

2. Mens Rea (Guilty Mind): Mens rea refers to the mental state or criminal intent of the offender at the time the actus reus was committed. It focuses on the accused's state of mind, emotions, and awareness while engaging in the criminal act. Mens rea can take various forms, including:

- Intention: The accused intended to cause a particular outcome or harm by their actions. Intent may be specific (aiming for a particular result) or general (aware of the probable consequences of the action).
- Recklessness: The accused acted recklessly, knowing there was a substantial risk that their actions could lead to harmful consequences.
- Negligence: The accused demonstrated negligence by failing to exercise reasonable care or caution, resulting in harm to others.
- Strict Liability: In some cases, mens rea may not be required if the offense is one of strict liability, meaning the act itself is sufficient to establish guilt regardless of the offender's mental state.

Mens rea is crucial in distinguishing between accidental actions and intentional criminal behavior. To prove criminal liability, the prosecution must establish that the accused possessed the necessary mental state to commit the crime.

Together, actus reus and mens rea form the basis of criminal liability. The prosecution must demonstrate that the accused committed a prohibited act (actus reus) with the required mental state (mens rea) to establish guilt beyond a reasonable doubt. These elements ensure that criminal liability is based on both the physical act and the criminal intent of the offender, promoting fairness and justice in criminal proceedings.

The principle of legality and retroactive laws

The principle of legality, also known as nullum crimen sine lege (no crime without law), is a fundamental legal principle in criminal law that dictates that an act can only be considered a crime if it is explicitly defined as such by law before the act was committed. This principle serves as a critical safeguard against arbitrariness and ensures that individuals are not subjected to punishment for conduct that was not prohibited by law at the time it occurred. Let's explore the principle of legality and its implications, particularly in relation to retroactive laws:

1. Principle of Legality: The principle of legality emphasizes the importance of legal certainty and predictability in criminal law. It requires that laws be clear, specific, and publicly accessible, so individuals can know in advance what conduct is criminal and what penalties may be imposed if they engage in such conduct. This principle is based on the idea that individuals should have fair notice of the consequences of their actions.

2. Prohibition of Retroactive Laws: The principle of legality prohibits the retroactive application of criminal laws. Retroactive laws, also known as ex post facto laws, are laws that are enacted after an act is committed and then applied to punish individuals for conduct that was legal when it occurred. In essence, retroactive laws change the legal consequences of actions taken before the laws were in effect.

3. Implications of Retroactive Laws: Retroactive laws are considered unjust and inconsistent with the principle

of legality for several reasons:

a. Fair Notice: Retroactive laws do not provide individuals with fair notice of what conduct is criminal and punishable, as the legal consequences are altered after the fact.

b. Punishment for Past Conduct: Applying retroactive laws allows the state to punish individuals for conduct that was lawful at the time it was committed. This undermines the notion that laws should be prospective and known to individuals before they act.

c. Protection against Abuse of Power: The prohibition of retroactive laws serves as a safeguard against potential abuse of legislative power. It prevents lawmakers from targeting specific individuals or groups by creating new laws after an event occurs to penalize them.

d. Legal Certainty: Retroactive laws create uncertainty in the legal system, as individuals may be unsure of their rights and obligations when laws can be changed retroactively.

e. Preserving the Rule of Law: The rule of law requires that laws be stable and predictable, ensuring that individuals are governed by pre-existing legal norms, not by laws created after their actions.

4. Exceptions: While retroactive criminal laws are generally prohibited, there are limited circumstances where retroactivity is allowed, such as when the retroactive application is favorable to the accused, or when it involves procedural or evidentiary matters that do not increase the penalty or punishment for the offense.

In summary, the principle of legality prohibits the retroactive application of criminal laws and emphasizes the importance of legal certainty and fairness in criminal justice systems. It ensures that individuals are not subjected to punishment for conduct that was not considered criminal at the time it occurred, upholding the fundamental principles of justice and the rule of law.

The concept of proportionality in sentencing

The concept of proportionality in sentencing is a fundamental principle in criminal law that seeks to ensure that the severity of the punishment imposed on an offender is proportionate to the seriousness of the crime committed. In other words, the punishment should fit the crime, reflecting a balanced and fair response to the wrongdoing. Proportionality in sentencing aims to achieve several objectives:

1. Justice and Fairness: Proportionality ensures that individuals who commit similar offenses receive similar sentences, promoting consistency and fairness in the criminal justice system. It prevents arbitrary or excessive punishment, safeguarding the rights of both victims and offenders.

2. Deterrence: A proportionate sentence serves as a deterrent, discouraging both the offender and others in society from engaging in similar criminal conduct. It sends a clear message about the consequences of illegal behavior and the seriousness with which society views certain offenses.

3. Rehabilitation: Proportionality takes into account the potential for rehabilitation and the possibility of reintegrating the offender back into society. A sentence that considers the offender's circumstances and the likelihood of rehabilitation may support successful reintegration and reduce the risk of recidivism.

4. Retribution: Proportionate sentences also address the concept of retributive justice, which seeks to mete

out a punishment proportionate to the harm caused by the offense. It acknowledges the moral and social debt incurred by the offender and seeks to balance it through appropriate punishment.

5. Respect for Human Dignity: A sentence that is excessive and disproportionate to the offense may violate the principle of human dignity, as it subjects the offender to unnecessary suffering beyond what is warranted by the crime.

It is important to note that the concept of proportionality does not imply that all crimes of a particular type should receive identical sentences. Rather, it recognizes that the gravity of offenses may vary based on factors such as the offender's level of culpability, the harm caused, the presence of aggravating or mitigating circumstances, and the impact on victims and society.

Courts consider various factors when determining a proportionate sentence, including the severity of the offense, the offender's criminal history, the circumstances of the crime, the degree of harm caused, the offender's remorse, and the potential for rehabilitation.

The application of proportionality in sentencing remains a delicate and complex task for judges and policymakers. Striking the right balance between the need for punishment, deterrence, rehabilitation, and respect for human rights is a continuous challenge in criminal justice systems around the world. However, upholding the principle of proportionality is crucial to maintaining a fair and just criminal justice system that respects the rights of all parties involved.

Criminal Law in Practice

Criminal law in practice involves the application of legal principles, statutes, and precedents to address criminal offenses and administer justice. It encompasses various stages, from the investigation and charging of suspects to trial, sentencing, and potential appeals. Here are some key aspects of criminal law in practice:

1. Investigation: Criminal investigations are conducted by law enforcement agencies to gather evidence, identify suspects, and build a case against individuals believed to have committed a crime. This stage may involve collecting witness statements, conducting searches, gathering forensic evidence, and interviewing suspects.

2. Charging: Once law enforcement believes they have sufficient evidence, they may forward the case to prosecutors. Prosecutors review the evidence to determine whether there is enough probable cause to file formal charges against the suspect. If so, the suspect is formally charged with the alleged offenses.

3. Pre-Trial Proceedings: Prior to the trial, there may be pre-trial proceedings, such as arraignment, where the accused enters a plea (guilty, not guilty, or no contest). Pre-trial motions may also be heard, addressing issues like admissibility of evidence or dismissal of charges.

4. Trial: During the trial, both the prosecution and defense present their cases, calling witnesses and presenting evidence. The judge or jury then deliberates on the facts and law to determine guilt or innocence.

Trials can be conducted by a judge (bench trial) or a jury (jury trial).

5. Sentencing: If the defendant is found guilty, the court proceeds to the sentencing phase. Sentencing considers various factors, such as the seriousness of the offense, the defendant's criminal history, and any mitigating or aggravating circumstances. The goal is to impose a proportionate and appropriate punishment.

6. Appeal: After a conviction, the defendant may have the right to appeal the decision to a higher court if they believe errors occurred during the trial that affected the outcome. Appellate courts review the trial proceedings, evidence, and legal arguments to determine whether the conviction should be upheld, modified, or overturned.

7. Alternatives to Trial: In some cases, criminal proceedings may be resolved through alternatives to trial, such as plea bargains or diversion programs. Plea bargains involve negotiations between the prosecution and defense, resulting in a guilty plea to reduced charges in exchange for a lighter sentence. Diversion programs offer rehabilitation and treatment options for certain offenders, allowing them to avoid formal criminal charges if they comply with specific conditions.

8. Corrections and Rehabilitation: After sentencing, offenders may serve their sentences in correctional facilities (prisons or jails) or be subject to probation or parole. Rehabilitation programs may also be provided to help offenders reintegrate into society and reduce the risk of reoffending.

Criminal law in practice is a complex and multifaceted process that aims to strike a balance between punishing criminal behavior, protecting public safety, upholding individual rights, and facilitating the potential for rehabilitation. Legal professionals, including judges, prosecutors, defense attorneys, and law enforcement officers, play critical roles in ensuring that criminal proceedings are conducted fairly and in accordance with the law.

The role of law enforcement in crime prevention and investigation

Law enforcement plays a crucial role in crime prevention and investigation to maintain public safety, uphold the rule of law, and protect communities from criminal activities. Their responsibilities encompass a range of proactive and reactive measures to address and deter criminal behavior. Here are the key roles of law enforcement in crime prevention and investigation:

1. Crime Prevention:
   - Patrols: Law enforcement officers conduct regular patrols in neighborhoods and public areas to deter criminal activities through their visible presence. Patrols help prevent crimes by deterring potential offenders and responding quickly to emerging threats.
   - Community Policing: Building strong relationships with communities fosters trust and cooperation between law enforcement and the public. Community policing initiatives encourage community involvement in crime prevention efforts and enable law enforcement to address local concerns effectively.
   - Crime Analysis: Law enforcement agencies use data analysis to identify crime patterns and hotspots. This information helps allocate resources strategically and target crime

prevention efforts in areas with higher crime rates.

- Public Education: Law enforcement agencies engage in public education campaigns to raise awareness about crime prevention strategies, safety measures, and reporting suspicious activities to the police.

2. Criminal Investigation:

- Evidence Collection: Law enforcement officers are responsible for collecting and preserving evidence at crime scenes. Proper handling of evidence is essential to build a solid case for prosecution.
- Interviews and Interrogations: Officers interview witnesses, victims, and suspects to gather information and elicit crucial details about the crime. Interrogations may be used to obtain confessions or additional information about the case.
- Forensic Analysis: Law enforcement agencies collaborate with forensic experts to analyze physical evidence, such as fingerprints, DNA, ballistics, and digital evidence, to link suspects to the crime.
- Surveillance and Undercover Operations: In certain cases, law enforcement may conduct surveillance or use undercover operations to gather evidence and monitor criminal activities discreetly.
- Collaborating with Prosecutors: Law enforcement works closely with prosecutors to ensure that the collected evidence meets legal standards and can support successful prosecution in court.

3. Crisis Response:

- Emergency Calls: Law enforcement responds

to emergency calls and situations, such as domestic disturbances, violent incidents, or accidents, to provide immediate assistance and maintain public safety.

- Crisis Negotiation: In situations involving hostage-taking or barricaded suspects, law enforcement may deploy crisis negotiation teams to defuse tense situations and achieve peaceful resolutions.

4. Arrest and Apprehension:

- When evidence points to a suspect's involvement in a crime, law enforcement officers may make arrests based on probable cause to bring the suspect into custody.
- Officers also execute arrest warrants issued by courts when suspects are wanted for specific criminal offenses.

Overall, law enforcement's proactive crime prevention efforts, combined with their diligent investigative work, are essential in reducing crime rates, identifying offenders, and fostering safer communities. Effective collaboration with the public, other law enforcement agencies, and criminal justice partners is crucial to fulfilling their mission in crime prevention and investigation.

Arrest, detention, and Miranda rights

Arrest, detention, and Miranda rights are critical components of the criminal justice system that safeguard individual rights and ensure due process for individuals suspected of committing crimes. Let's explore each of these concepts in detail:

1. Arrest:

   - An arrest occurs when a law enforcement officer takes a person into custody, intending to deprive them of their freedom. It is usually based on probable cause, which means the officer has reasonable grounds to believe that the person committed a crime. Arrests can be made with or without a warrant, depending on the circumstances and the seriousness of the offense.
   - During an arrest, law enforcement officers must inform the individual of the reason for the arrest, known as the "grounds of arrest" or "cause for arrest." This helps the arrested person understand the basis for their detention.
   - After the arrest, the person is taken to a police station or detention facility for booking, where personal information is recorded, and the charges are officially entered into the system.

2. Detention:

   - Detention refers to the period during which a person is held in custody after being arrested. It is a temporary state of confinement pending further investigation or the resolution of legal proceedings.

- Detention should not be indefinite or without justification. Authorities must promptly bring the detained person before a court, where the legality of the detention will be reviewed. If the court finds the detention unlawful, the person must be released.

3. Miranda Rights:

- Miranda rights stem from the landmark U.S. Supreme Court case Miranda v. Arizona (1966). They are a set of constitutional rights that must be read to an arrested individual before any custodial interrogation takes place.
- The Miranda warning typically includes the following rights:
  - The right to remain silent: The individual has the right to refuse to answer questions and avoid self-incrimination.
  - Anything they say can and will be used against them in court: Any statements made by the individual during the interrogation may be used as evidence in subsequent legal proceedings.
  - The right to an attorney: The individual has the right to have an attorney present during the interrogation. If they cannot afford an attorney, one will be provided at no cost (the right to a public defender).
  - The right to stop the questioning at any time: The individual can choose to exercise their right to remain silent at

    any point during the interrogation.

- The purpose of the Miranda warning is to inform the arrested person of their constitutional rights, particularly the Fifth Amendment right against self-incrimination and the Sixth Amendment right to counsel. It ensures that any statements made by the individual during custodial interrogation are made voluntarily and with an understanding of their legal rights.
- If law enforcement fails to provide the Miranda warning when required, any statements made during custodial interrogation may be deemed inadmissible as evidence in court.

Arrest, detention, and the administration of Miranda rights are essential aspects of protecting individual rights and ensuring that criminal investigations and proceedings are conducted fairly and in accordance with the law. These safeguards help maintain the integrity of the criminal justice system and uphold the principle of due process for all individuals, whether they are suspects or defendants.

Criminal trials and the adversarial process

Criminal trials in many legal systems, including common law jurisdictions like the United States, follow an adversarial process. The adversarial process is a legal system where two opposing parties—the prosecution and the defense—present evidence and arguments to an impartial judge or jury. Let's explore the key features and stages of a criminal trial under the adversarial process:

1. Pre-Trial Proceedings:
   - Arrest and Booking: The pre-trial process begins with the arrest and booking of the suspect. The suspect is informed of the charges against them and may be granted bail or detained pending trial.
   - Arraignment: The accused is brought before a court for arraignment, where they are formally informed of the charges against them and asked to enter a plea (guilty, not guilty, or no contest).
   - Discovery: During the pre-trial phase, both the prosecution and defense exchange information and evidence relevant to the case in a process known as discovery.
2. Trial Preparation:
   - Jury Selection: In cases with a jury trial, potential jurors are selected through a process called voir dire, where both sides question potential jurors to ensure an impartial jury.
   - Motions: Before the trial begins, both the

prosecution and defense may file motions, asking the court to make rulings on specific legal issues or evidence admissibility.

3. Trial:

- Opening Statements: Both the prosecution and defense present their opening statements to outline their theories of the case and what they intend to prove.
- Presentation of Evidence: The prosecution presents its case first, calling witnesses, presenting physical evidence, and introducing exhibits. The defense has the opportunity to cross-examine prosecution witnesses.
- Cross-Examination: After the prosecution's direct examination, the defense has the opportunity to cross-examine witnesses to challenge their testimony or credibility.
- Closing Arguments: After all evidence is presented, both sides deliver closing arguments summarizing their case and urging the judge or jury to find in their favor.
- Jury Instructions: The judge provides instructions to the jury regarding the relevant law and legal standards they must apply when deliberating on the verdict.

4. Verdict:

- Jury Deliberation: In jury trials, the jury retreats to a private room to deliberate on the evidence presented and reach a verdict. In bench trials (trials without a jury), the judge issues the verdict.
- Verdict: The jury (or judge) returns to the courtroom and announces the verdict, either "guilty" or "not guilty."

5. Sentencing (if applicable):

- If the verdict is "guilty," a separate sentencing phase follows, where the judge determines the appropriate punishment based on sentencing guidelines and any mitigating or aggravating factors presented by both sides.

The adversarial process is designed to allow each side to vigorously advocate for their position and present their evidence, subject to rules of evidence and procedural fairness. The judge or jury serves as an impartial decision-maker, responsible for determining guilt or innocence based on the evidence and legal standards presented during the trial.

This process emphasizes the importance of advocacy, due process, and the rights of the accused, aiming to ensure a fair and transparent resolution of criminal cases. While the adversarial process has its strengths, it also has limitations, and some legal systems incorporate elements of an inquisitorial approach to complement the adversarial model and seek a more comprehensive understanding of the truth in complex cases.

The role of legal professionals: judges, prosecutors, and defense attorneys

Legal professionals, including judges, prosecutors, and defense attorneys, play vital roles in the criminal justice system. Each of these professionals has distinct responsibilities and functions that contribute to the fair and effective administration of justice. Let's explore the roles of each:

1. Judges:
   - Impartial Decision-Making: Judges are impartial and neutral decision-makers who preside over criminal trials and hearings. They ensure that legal proceedings are conducted fairly and in accordance with the law.
   - Rulings on Legal Issues: Judges make determinations on various legal matters, such as admissibility of evidence, motions filed by the prosecution or defense, and objections during the trial.
   - Sentencing: If the defendant is found guilty, judges are responsible for determining the appropriate punishment within the framework of sentencing guidelines and statutory provisions.

2. Prosecutors:
   - Representing the State: Prosecutors, also known as district attorneys or state attorneys, represent the government (state or

federal) in criminal cases. Their role is to present evidence and arguments against the defendant to prove guilt beyond a reasonable doubt.

- Charging Decisions: Prosecutors review evidence gathered by law enforcement and decide whether to bring formal charges (file a complaint or indictment) against the accused based on the strength of the case.
- Plea Negotiations: In many cases, prosecutors engage in plea negotiations with the defense to reach a plea agreement, whereby the defendant may plead guilty to reduced charges in exchange for a lighter sentence.

3. Defense Attorneys:

- Legal Representation: Defense attorneys represent the accused and advocate for their rights throughout the criminal proceedings.
- Ensuring Due Process: Defense attorneys ensure that the defendant's constitutional rights are protected and that they receive a fair trial.
- Investigating the Case: Defense attorneys conduct their own investigation, gather evidence, and interview witnesses to build a defense strategy.
- Presenting the Defense: During the trial, defense attorneys cross-examine prosecution witnesses, present evidence in support of the defendant's case, and make arguments challenging the prosecution's case.

Overall, the roles of judges, prosecutors, and defense attorneys are critical to maintaining a balance between the interests of the state in prosecuting criminal offenses and safeguarding the rights of individuals accused of crimes. Their work contributes to the integrity of the criminal justice system, ensuring that the accused receives a fair trial, that evidence is presented and evaluated properly, and that justice is served in a manner that respects the rule of law and due process.

Criminal Offenses and their Classifications

Criminal offenses can be classified into different categories based on their severity and the potential punishment they carry. The classifications vary from one legal system to another, but common categories include:

1. Felonies:
   - Felonies are serious criminal offenses that typically carry severe penalties, including imprisonment for more than one year, significant fines, or both.
   - Examples of felonies include murder, manslaughter, rape, robbery, burglary, kidnapping, certain drug offenses, and white-collar crimes like embezzlement and fraud.

2. Misdemeanors:
   - Misdemeanors are less serious offenses than felonies but are still punishable by imprisonment for up to one year, fines, probation, community service, or other forms of punishment.
   - Examples of misdemeanors include simple assault, petty theft, disorderly conduct, certain drug possession offenses, and some traffic violations.

3. Infractions (Violations):
   - Infractions, also known as violations or petty offenses, are minor offenses that are typically punishable by fines, community service, or other minor penalties, but not imprisonment.

- Examples of infractions include minor traffic offenses, littering, public intoxication, and some minor drug offenses.

4. Capital Offenses (in some jurisdictions):
   - Capital offenses are crimes that carry the possibility of the death penalty as a potential punishment. These offenses are the most serious crimes, often involving premeditated murder or aggravated circumstances.
   - The death penalty is not universally accepted, and not all jurisdictions impose it. In many places, there has been a growing trend toward abolishing or placing moratoriums on capital punishment.

5. Wobblers (in some jurisdictions):
   - Some offenses are classified as "wobblers" because they can be charged as either misdemeanors or felonies, depending on the specific circumstances of the case and the prosecutor's discretion. The classification may be influenced by factors such as the defendant's criminal history and the severity of the offense.

It's important to note that the classification of offenses may vary from one jurisdiction to another, as each country or state establishes its own criminal code and sentencing guidelines. Additionally, some legal systems may use different terminology or further subdivide offenses based on various factors. The classification of offenses helps provide a framework for determining appropriate penalties and ensuring a fair and consistent application of the law.

Overview of different types of criminal offenses (e.g., violent crimes, property crimes, white-collar crimes)

Criminal offenses can be broadly categorized into various types based on the nature of the offense and the harm it causes to individuals or society. Here's an overview of different types of criminal offenses:

1. Violent Crimes:
   - Violent crimes involve the use of force or the threat of force against another person, causing physical harm or the fear of harm. Examples include:
     - Homicide: Murder (intentional killing) and manslaughter (unintentional killing).
     - Assault: Physically attacking or threatening to harm another person.
     - Robbery: Using force, threats, or intimidation to steal property from another person.
2. Property Crimes:
   - Property crimes involve offenses against property, where the intention is to deprive the owner of their possessions without using force against a person. Examples include:
     - Theft: Taking someone's property without their consent.

- Burglary: Illegally entering a building or structure with the intent to commit a crime (often theft).
- Arson: Deliberately setting fire to property.

3. White-Collar Crimes:
   - White-collar crimes are non-violent offenses typically committed by individuals in business, government, or professional settings for financial gain. Examples include:
     - Fraud: Deception to obtain money, property, or services dishonestly.
     - Embezzlement: Misappropriating funds or property entrusted to one's care.
     - Bribery: Offering or accepting money, gifts, or favors to influence official actions.

4. Drug Offenses:
   - Drug offenses involve the illegal possession, manufacturing, distribution, or trafficking of controlled substances. Drug offenses vary in severity depending on the type and quantity of drugs involved.

5. Cybercrimes:
   - Cybercrimes are offenses committed using computers, networks, or the internet. Examples include hacking, identity theft, and cyberstalking.

6. Sex Crimes:
   - Sex crimes involve sexual offenses against individuals, including:
     - Sexual Assault: Non-consensual sexual contact or activity.
     - Rape: Non-consensual sexual intercourse.

- Child Sexual Abuse: Sexual offenses committed against minors.

7. Public Order Crimes:
    - Public order crimes involve behaviors that disturb public peace and order. Examples include:
        - Public Intoxication: Being intoxicated in public.
        - Disorderly Conduct: Engaging in disruptive or offensive behavior in public.

8. Traffic Offenses:
    - Traffic offenses include violations of traffic laws and regulations, such as speeding, driving under the influence (DUI), and reckless driving.

9. Juvenile Offenses:
    - Juvenile offenses are committed by individuals who are under the age of majority (usually 18). These offenses are handled in juvenile court and may include various types of criminal behavior.

These are just a few examples of the different types of criminal offenses. The classification and specific definitions of offenses can vary between jurisdictions, and some jurisdictions may have additional or different categories of crimes based on their legal systems and societal norms. The criminal justice system aims to hold individuals accountable for their actions while ensuring a fair and just process for both the accused and victims.

Felonies, misdemeanors, and their consequences

Felonies and misdemeanors are two main categories of criminal offenses, distinguished primarily by the severity of the offense and the potential punishment they carry. The consequences for each category can vary significantly, as outlined below:

1. Felonies:
   - Felonies are serious criminal offenses and typically involve more significant harm to individuals or society. Examples include murder, robbery, rape, arson, and certain drug offenses.
   - Consequences:
     - Imprisonment: Felonies often carry sentences of more than one year in prison, ranging from several years to life imprisonment or, in some cases, the death penalty (in jurisdictions where capital punishment is permitted).
     - Fines: Convicted felons may face substantial fines as part of their sentence, which can amount to thousands or even millions of dollars, depending on the offense.
     - Loss of Civil Rights: Convicted felons may lose certain civil rights, such as the right to vote, serve on a jury,

or possess firearms, depending on the jurisdiction.

- Collateral Consequences: Felony convictions can have far-reaching consequences beyond the formal punishment, including difficulties in obtaining employment, housing, and professional licenses.

2. Misdemeanors:

- Misdemeanors are less serious offenses compared to felonies but are still considered crimes. Examples include simple assault, petty theft, disorderly conduct, and some drug possession offenses.
- Consequences:
  - Imprisonment: Misdemeanors generally carry shorter jail sentences of up to one year, but the actual sentence can vary depending on the jurisdiction and the specific offense.
  - Fines: Convicted individuals may be required to pay fines as part of their punishment. The fines for misdemeanors are typically lower than those for felonies.
  - Probation: In some cases, offenders may be placed on probation instead of serving jail time. Probation typically involves supervision, adherence to certain conditions, and regular check-ins with a probation officer.
  - Community Service: Courts may order individuals to perform community service as an alternative or in addition to other penalties.

The categorization of offenses as felonies or misdemeanors and the specific consequences associated with each category vary based on the laws of each jurisdiction. In some jurisdictions, certain offenses may be classified as "wobblers," allowing prosecutors to charge them as either felonies or misdemeanors based on the circumstances of the case and the defendant's criminal history.

It's important to note that criminal justice systems prioritize fair and proportionate punishment while also considering factors such as the defendant's criminal record, the circumstances of the offense, and any mitigating or aggravating factors during sentencing. The goal is to ensure that the punishment is commensurate with the seriousness of the offense and to promote rehabilitation and deterrence while upholding individual rights and the principles of justice.

Emerging crimes in the digital age (e.g., cybercrime, identity theft)

The digital age has brought about significant advancements in technology, communication, and connectivity. While these developments have revolutionized various aspects of society, they have also given rise to new forms of crime known as cybercrimes. Here are some examples of emerging crimes in the digital age:

1. Cybercrime:
    - Cybercrime encompasses a wide range of offenses committed using computers, the internet, or digital devices. Examples include:
        - Hacking: Unauthorized access to computer systems or networks to steal information or disrupt operations.
        - Phishing: Sending deceptive emails or messages to trick individuals into revealing sensitive information, such as passwords or financial details.
        - Ransomware: Malicious software that encrypts files on a victim's computer, with cybercriminals demanding a ransom for decryption.
        - Cyberbullying: Harassing, threatening, or intimidating others online, often through social media platforms or messaging apps.
        - Online Fraud: Engaging in fraudulent

activities, such as online auctions scams, investment schemes, or fake online marketplaces.

2. Identity Theft:
  - Identity theft involves stealing someone's personal information (e.g., Social Security number, credit card details) to impersonate them or commit fraud.
  - Synthetic Identity Theft: Creating new identities by combining real and fake information to deceive financial institutions and commit fraud.

3. Online Harassment and Stalking:
  - Harassment and stalking have extended to the digital realm, with individuals using social media, emails, or messaging apps to target and torment others.

4. Cyber Espionage:
  - Nation-states and hackers engage in cyber espionage to steal sensitive information, trade secrets, or intellectual property from governments, corporations, or individuals.

5. Cyber Extortion:
  - Cyber extortion involves threats or demands made online, usually accompanied by the threat of releasing sensitive or damaging information unless a ransom is paid.

6. Deepfake Technology Misuse:
  - Deepfake technology allows the creation of manipulated videos and audios that can make individuals appear to say or do things they never did, leading to potential misuse and misinformation.

7. Virtual Currency Crimes:
  - With the rise of cryptocurrencies, criminals exploit them for illicit activities, such as

money laundering, tax evasion, and ransom payments in cybercrimes.

8. Internet of Things (IoT) Vulnerabilities:
   - The increased use of IoT devices presents security challenges, as hackers may exploit vulnerabilities in these devices for malicious purposes.

Addressing these emerging crimes requires continuous efforts from law enforcement, cybersecurity professionals, and policymakers. It involves developing effective cybersecurity measures, educating the public about online safety, and establishing legal frameworks to prosecute cybercriminals. Additionally, international cooperation and information sharing are essential to combat cyber threats effectively in an interconnected digital world.

The Evolution of Punishment and Correctional Systems

The evolution of punishment and correctional systems throughout history has been influenced by changes in societal attitudes, philosophical perspectives on justice, and advancements in governance and technology. Let's explore the major stages of this evolution:

1. Retribution and Vengeance:
   - In ancient societies, punishment was often driven by a desire for vengeance and retribution. It focused on inflicting pain or harm on wrongdoers as a means of balancing the scales of justice and appeasing victims or their families.
   - Punishments during this era included physical forms of retribution, such as public floggings, mutilation, or even death penalties, which were often harsh and lacked considerations of proportionality.
2. Restorative Justice:
   - Over time, societies started recognizing the need for restoration and reconciliation rather than pure retribution. Restorative justice emphasized repairing the harm caused by crimes and facilitating healing for both victims and offenders.
   - Community-based approaches, such as mediation and restitution, aimed at involving

all stakeholders in the resolution of conflicts and promoting accountability.

3. Incarceration and the Penitentiary System:
   - The emergence of the penitentiary system in the 18th and 19th centuries marked a significant shift in punishment methods. The idea was to reform offenders through penance, reflection, and isolation from society.
   - The first modern penitentiaries, like Philadelphia's Eastern State Penitentiary, implemented the concept of solitary confinement and labor, with the belief that time for reflection and work would lead to repentance.

4. Rehabilitation:
   - The 20th century saw a greater emphasis on rehabilitation as a primary goal of correctional systems. The idea was to reform offenders through education, vocational training, and therapy to prepare them for reintegration into society.
   - Programs focusing on drug rehabilitation, mental health treatment, and job training were introduced to address underlying issues contributing to criminal behavior.

5. Deterrence and Incapacitation:
   - Alongside rehabilitation, deterrence and incapacitation became influential goals in punishment philosophy. Deterrence aims to dissuade potential offenders by imposing punishments severe enough to discourage criminal behavior.
   - Incapacitation involves removing dangerous individuals from society to prevent them from committing further crimes. This may

take the form of lengthy prison sentences or even life imprisonment for violent offenders.

6. Restorative Justice Reemergence:
   - In recent years, there has been a renewed interest in restorative justice approaches. Advocates argue that focusing on repairing harm, promoting dialogue between victims and offenders, and involving communities can lead to more meaningful and long-lasting resolutions.

7. Advancements in Rehabilitation:
   - Advances in psychology and behavioral sciences have influenced correctional systems to adopt evidence-based rehabilitation programs tailored to individual needs.
   - Cognitive-behavioral therapy, substance abuse treatment, and educational programs are now common components of many correctional facilities.

8. Alternatives to Incarceration:
   - Recognizing the limitations of traditional incarceration, there has been a growing emphasis on alternatives to imprisonment, such as probation, parole, electronic monitoring, and diversion programs for non-violent offenders.

The evolution of punishment and correctional systems reflects an ongoing search for more effective and just ways of dealing with criminal behavior. Modern approaches strive to strike a balance between punishment, rehabilitation, deterrence, and restoration while considering the complexities of individual circumstances and societal needs.

Historical approaches to punishment and retribution

Historical approaches to punishment and retribution have evolved significantly over time, reflecting the prevailing cultural, religious, and philosophical beliefs of different societies. Here are some key historical approaches to punishment and retribution:

1. Blood Feuds and Eye for an Eye:
     - In ancient societies, particularly tribal and early feudal systems, retaliation was a common form of punishment. The principle of "an eye for an eye" or "lex talionis" prevailed, where the punishment for a crime mirrored the harm caused to the victim or their family.
     - Blood feuds involved cycles of revenge killings between families or clans, perpetuating violence and retribution.
2. Corporal Punishment and Public Spectacles:
     - During medieval times, corporal punishment was widespread and often carried out publicly as a form of deterrence and retribution. Offenders could be subjected to public whippings, branding, or even mutilation as punishment for their crimes.
     - Public executions, such as beheadings, hangings, or burning at the stake, were also common spectacles designed to instill

fear in the populace and demonstrate the consequences of defying the law.

3. Ordeals and Trial by Combat:

- In some societies, particularly during the early Middle Ages, ordeals and trial by combat were used as forms of divine judgment to determine guilt or innocence. Ordeals involved physical tests, such as carrying hot iron or plunging a hand into boiling water, with the belief that divine intervention would protect the innocent.
- Trial by combat allowed the accused and the accuser to resolve their dispute through a duel, with the winner considered vindicated by God.

4. Banishment and Exile:

- Banishment and exile were common forms of punishment during various historical periods. Offenders were forced to leave their communities, often as a means of removing potential threats or as a form of public shame.

5. Torture:

- Torture was used in many societies as a means of extracting confessions or information from suspects. Methods ranged from beatings and waterboarding to more elaborate and painful techniques.

6. Restitution and Compensatory Justice:

- In some ancient civilizations, such as Mesopotamia, the concept of restitution played a role in criminal justice. Offenders were required to compensate victims or their families as a form of retribution and to restore balance in society.

7. Religious Punishments:

- In societies where religion played a central

role, punishments were often aligned with religious beliefs and doctrines. Punishments could be seen as divine retribution for sinful behavior, reflecting the concept of divine justice.

As societies evolved and developed more complex legal systems, approaches to punishment and retribution shifted toward more organized, structured, and codified systems of law. Concepts of justice, rehabilitation, and the balance between the rights of the individual and the needs of society gradually emerged, leading to the development of modern criminal justice systems that aim to achieve justice while upholding principles of fairness and humanity.

Modern theories of punishment: retribution, deterrence, rehabilitation, and incapacitation

Modern theories of punishment aim to achieve various objectives in the criminal justice system. These theories form the basis for determining the appropriate form and severity of punishment for criminal offenders. Here are four key modern theories of punishment:

1. Retribution:
    - Retributive justice focuses on the idea of proportionate punishment as a means of retribution for the harm caused by the offender's actions. It aims to restore the balance of justice by inflicting a punishment equal to the severity of the crime committed.
    - The underlying principle is that offenders deserve punishment for their wrongdoing, regardless of any potential benefits or deterrent effects. It upholds the concept of individual responsibility and the idea that society has a right to see justice served.
2. Deterrence:
    - The deterrence theory emphasizes the preventive aspect of punishment. It posits that the threat of punishment can deter individuals from committing crimes in the first place.
    - There are two types of deterrence:
        - General Deterrence: This aims to

discourage the general public from committing crimes by demonstrating the consequences faced by offenders.

- Specific Deterrence: This focuses on deterring individual offenders from re-offending by imposing punishments severe enough to dissuade them from future criminal behavior.

3. Rehabilitation:

- The rehabilitation theory centers on the idea that offenders can be reformed or rehabilitated through various interventions and treatment programs.
- It views criminal behavior as a result of social, psychological, or environmental factors, and aims to address these underlying issues to reduce the likelihood of future criminal activity.
- Rehabilitation programs may include education, vocational training, counseling, drug treatment, and mental health support.

4. Incapacitation:

- Incapacitation theory seeks to protect society from further harm by removing dangerous offenders from the community.
- The focus is on physically separating offenders from society through imprisonment or other means, preventing them from committing additional crimes during their incarceration.
- The goal is to reduce the risk of recidivism and protect public safety.

In practice, the criminal justice system often combines these theories to varying degrees, depending on the jurisdiction, the nature of the offense, and the offender's individual circumstances. For instance, some countries may prioritize rehabilitation for non-violent offenders while emphasizing deterrence and incapacitation for violent or repeat offenders.

The debate over which theory of punishment is most effective and just remains ongoing, and many believe that a balanced approach that considers the goals of retribution, deterrence, rehabilitation, and incapacitation can lead to a more comprehensive and fair criminal justice system.

The role of restorative justice and its impact on criminal sentencing

Restorative justice is an alternative approach to addressing criminal behavior that focuses on repairing the harm caused by the offense, promoting healing for victims, holding offenders accountable, and engaging the community in the resolution process. The goal of restorative justice is to achieve reconciliation and restore relationships between the parties involved. Its impact on criminal sentencing can be significant, influencing both the process and outcomes of sentencing. Here's how restorative justice affects criminal sentencing:

1. Victim Participation:
   - Restorative justice gives victims a more active role in the criminal justice process. They have the opportunity to express their feelings, share the impact of the crime on their lives, and have their needs and concerns heard by both the offender and the broader community.
   - This direct involvement allows victims to have a say in the terms of the resolution, potentially leading to outcomes that focus on restitution, apologies, or other actions aimed at repairing the harm done.

2. Offender Accountability:
   - Restorative justice emphasizes holding offenders accountable for their actions in a more meaningful way. By facing the

consequences of their behavior and engaging with victims, offenders gain a better understanding of the harm they caused and the impact of their actions.

. Offenders are encouraged to take responsibility for their behavior, make amends, and actively participate in the process of repairing the harm.

3. Community Involvement:

. Restorative justice involves the community in the resolution process. Community members, along with victims and offenders, may participate in circles, conferences, or mediation sessions.

. Community involvement strengthens social bonds, fosters empathy, and reinforces the idea that crime affects not only individuals but also the broader community.

4. Individualized Sentencing:

. Restorative justice approaches allow for more individualized sentencing based on the unique circumstances of each case. Sentencing decisions take into account the specific needs and interests of victims, as well as the willingness of offenders to take responsibility for their actions and make amends.

. This flexibility can lead to creative and contextually appropriate outcomes that go beyond traditional punitive measures.

5. Reduced Recidivism:

. Studies have suggested that restorative justice practices can contribute to lower rates of recidivism compared to traditional punitive approaches. By addressing the underlying causes of criminal behavior and fostering rehabilitation and reintegration, restorative justice may break the cycle of crime and encourage positive change in offenders.

6. Challenges and Limitations:

- Restorative justice is not suitable for all cases, particularly those involving serious or violent offenses, or when victims are not willing or able to participate in the process.
- Implementing restorative justice requires the support and cooperation of various stakeholders, including criminal justice officials, community members, and support services.

Overall, restorative justice offers an alternative framework for addressing criminal behavior that prioritizes healing, accountability, and community involvement. When integrated effectively into the criminal justice system, restorative justice can complement traditional punitive measures and contribute to a more balanced and victim-centered approach to sentencing.

Challenges in the Criminal Justice System

The criminal justice system faces numerous challenges that impact its effectiveness, fairness, and ability to serve the needs of society. Some of the key challenges include:

1. Overcrowded Prisons and Mass Incarceration:
    - Many countries struggle with overcrowded prisons, leading to substandard living conditions for inmates and limited resources for rehabilitation and support services.
    - Mass incarceration, often driven by harsh sentencing laws and punitive policies, poses significant challenges in managing and addressing the needs of a large inmate population.
2. Racial and Socioeconomic Disparities:
    - Racial and socioeconomic disparities exist at various stages of the criminal justice process, from policing and arrests to sentencing and incarceration.
    - Minority and economically disadvantaged individuals are disproportionately affected by these disparities, leading to a lack of trust in the system and perceptions of injustice.
3. Access to Legal Representation:
    - Many individuals, especially those from lower-income backgrounds, face challenges accessing competent legal representation.

This can lead to inadequate defense, potential miscarriages of justice, and an imbalance of power in court proceedings.

4. Backlog of Cases and Delayed Justice:
   - Overloaded court systems and procedural complexities can result in significant delays in the resolution of cases. Lengthy delays can undermine the integrity of the justice system and cause additional stress for victims, witnesses, and defendants.

5. Lack of Rehabilitation and Reintegration Programs:
   - Inadequate resources for rehabilitation and reintegration programs can hinder efforts to address the underlying causes of criminal behavior and support successful reintegration into society after incarceration.
   - Limited access to education, vocational training, mental health services, and substance abuse treatment may contribute to higher rates of recidivism.

6. Use of Pretrial Detention:
   - Excessive reliance on pretrial detention can lead to individuals being held in jail before their trials for extended periods, even for minor offenses. This can disproportionately affect those unable to afford bail and contribute to the presumption of guilt before trial.

7. Police Accountability and Use of Force:
   - Instances of police misconduct and the inappropriate use of force by law enforcement have raised concerns about accountability and trust between communities and the police.
   - Calls for police reform and improved training to reduce the use of excessive force have

become significant issues.
8. Technological Challenges:
   - Rapid advancements in technology pose challenges in handling digital evidence, ensuring data privacy, and addressing cybercrimes effectively.
9. Lack of Restorative Justice Practices:
   - Despite the benefits of restorative justice, its implementation remains limited in many jurisdictions. The adoption of alternative dispute resolution methods and restorative practices can be slow due to resistance or lack of resources.

Addressing these challenges requires collaborative efforts from policymakers, criminal justice professionals, communities, and advocacy groups. Striving for reform and improvements in areas such as sentencing policies, access to legal representation, rehabilitation programs, and community policing can lead to a more equitable and effective criminal justice system.

Addressing systemic biases and promoting equal treatment

Addressing systemic biases and promoting equal treatment within the criminal justice system is essential for creating a fair and just society. Here are some strategies and initiatives that can help achieve these goals:

1. Data Collection and Analysis:
   - Collect and analyze comprehensive data on arrests, sentencing, and incarceration rates to identify and address racial and socioeconomic disparities.
   - Implement policies that require transparency in reporting and accountability for bias-related issues.
2. Implicit Bias Training:
   - Provide training for law enforcement, judges, prosecutors, and other criminal justice professionals to recognize and address implicit biases that may influence decision-making.
   - Raise awareness about the potential impact of biases on individual judgments and actions.
3. Community Policing and Engagement:
   - Encourage community policing practices that prioritize building positive relationships between law enforcement and the communities they serve.
   - Involve community members in the

development of policing policies and practices to ensure they are responsive to community needs.

4. Fair and Equitable Sentencing:
   - Promote sentencing reforms that focus on proportionality and individualized justice rather than relying solely on mandatory minimums or one-size-fits-all approaches.
   - Provide judges with discretion to consider the unique circumstances of each case, including mitigating factors and rehabilitation prospects.

5. Bail Reform:
   - Implement bail reform measures that prioritize risk assessment over financial considerations, reducing the disproportionate impact on economically disadvantaged individuals.
   - Utilize pretrial services to assess flight risk and public safety concerns rather than relying on monetary bail.

6. Alternatives to Incarceration:
   - Invest in diversion programs, specialty courts (e.g., drug courts, mental health courts), and restorative justice practices that address underlying issues and promote rehabilitation instead of solely relying on incarceration.

7. Access to Legal Representation:
   - Ensure access to quality legal representation for all individuals, particularly those from vulnerable communities or low-income backgrounds.
   - Implement public defender programs and other initiatives to improve the quality of defense provided to indigent defendants.

8. Diverse Judiciary and Criminal Justice Workforce:

- Promote diversity and inclusion within the criminal justice system, including recruiting and retaining a diverse workforce of judges, prosecutors, defense attorneys, and law enforcement officers.
- Diverse perspectives can help mitigate biases and contribute to more equitable decision-making.

9. Reentry Support:
   - Offer comprehensive reentry programs to support formerly incarcerated individuals in their transition back into society, providing access to housing, employment opportunities, and social services to reduce recidivism.

10. Community-Based Solutions:
   - Partner with community organizations, advocates, and stakeholders to develop collaborative solutions that address specific issues affecting marginalized communities.
   - Empower communities to play a role in the design and implementation of initiatives aimed at promoting equal treatment and reducing systemic biases.

Addressing systemic biases and promoting equal treatment requires ongoing commitment and collaboration from all stakeholders within the criminal justice system and the broader community. By taking proactive measures and implementing evidence-based practices, it is possible to create a more equitable and effective criminal justice system that upholds the principles of justice for all.

Ensuring access to legal representation and legal aid

Ensuring access to legal representation and legal aid is crucial for upholding the principles of justice and fairness in the criminal justice system. Adequate legal representation is essential to protect the rights of individuals, particularly those who may face economic or social barriers. Here are some ways to ensure access to legal representation and legal aid:

1. Public Defender Programs:
   - Establish and fund public defender programs that provide legal representation to individuals who cannot afford private attorneys. Public defenders are crucial in protecting the rights of indigent defendants and ensuring a fair trial.
2. Legal Aid Organizations:
   - Support and fund legal aid organizations that offer free or low-cost legal services to individuals in need. These organizations often cater to vulnerable populations, including low-income individuals, minorities, immigrants, and victims of domestic violence.
3. Pro Bono Services:
   - Encourage private attorneys to offer pro bono (free) legal services to those who cannot afford representation. Bar associations and legal organizations can promote pro bono

work and recognize attorneys who contribute their time and expertise.

4. Means Testing:
   - Implement means testing to determine eligibility for free or subsidized legal representation. This ensures that legal aid resources are directed to those who truly need them.

5. Court-Appointed Attorneys:
   - In cases where legal representation is required, but the defendant cannot afford an attorney, courts can appoint counsel to ensure representation.
   - The appointment of counsel is particularly critical in criminal cases, where the accused's liberty is at stake.

6. Expanded Legal Aid Coverage:
   - Advocate for expanded legal aid coverage to address a broader range of legal issues, including housing, family law, immigration, and employment disputes.
   - Access to legal aid for civil matters is essential for protecting individuals from injustices in non-criminal contexts.

7. Online Resources and Self-Help Tools:
   - Develop online resources and self-help tools to assist individuals with legal information and forms, making legal processes more accessible and understandable.

8. Mobile Legal Clinics:
   - Establish mobile legal clinics that reach underserved communities, especially those in remote or economically disadvantaged areas.
   - These clinics can provide legal advice and assistance on various legal matters.

9. Legal Education and Awareness:

- Promote legal education and awareness initiatives to inform individuals about their rights and available legal resources.
- Empower communities to better navigate the legal system and seek appropriate legal aid when needed.

10. Collaboration and Funding:

- Foster collaboration between government agencies, nonprofits, law firms, and other stakeholders to improve the coordination of legal aid services and secure sustainable funding.

By implementing these measures, societies can work toward ensuring that everyone, regardless of their financial status, has access to competent legal representation. Access to legal aid is not only a matter of justice but also vital for maintaining the integrity and fairness of the legal system as a whole.

Overcoming obstacles in the investigation and prosecution of crimes

Overcoming obstacles in the investigation and prosecution of crimes is essential to ensure that justice is served and perpetrators are held accountable. Several challenges can impede the successful investigation and prosecution of crimes. Here are some strategies to address these obstacles:

1. Insufficient Resources:
   - Increase funding and resources for law enforcement agencies and prosecutors to enhance their investigative capabilities and capacity to handle cases effectively.
   - Adequate resources can lead to better training, equipment, and technology, which can improve the quality and efficiency of investigations.
2. Witness Cooperation and Protection:
   - Establish witness protection programs to encourage cooperation from witnesses, especially in high-profile or dangerous cases.
   - Ensure that witnesses feel safe and supported throughout the legal process to prevent intimidation or fear of retaliation.
3. Forensic Evidence and Technology:
   - Invest in modern forensic technologies and expertise to improve the collection, analysis, and presentation of evidence in court.
   - Promote the use of advanced technologies

such as DNA analysis, digital forensics, and surveillance techniques to strengthen cases.

4. Lack of Cooperation and Communication:

- Foster better communication and cooperation between law enforcement agencies, prosecutors, and other relevant stakeholders.
- Encourage collaboration and information sharing to facilitate seamless coordination during investigations and prosecutions.

5. Handling Complex Cases:

- Establish specialized units or task forces to handle complex and challenging cases, such as organized crime, financial fraud, or cybercrimes.
- These units can pool expertise and resources to tackle intricate investigations effectively.

6. Backlog of Cases:

- Implement measures to reduce case backlogs and ensure timely processing of cases through improved case management systems and court efficiency.
- Prioritize cases based on seriousness and potential impact on public safety.

7. Addressing Witness Intimidation:

- Enforce laws and implement policies that protect witnesses from intimidation and harassment, ensuring that they feel safe to come forward with information.
- Prosecute those who attempt to obstruct justice or tamper with witnesses.

8. Language Barriers and Cultural Sensitivity:

- Train law enforcement officers and prosecutors to be culturally sensitive and equipped to communicate effectively with diverse communities.

- Provide language interpretation services to overcome language barriers that might hinder investigations.

9. Public Cooperation and Trust:
   - Build trust between law enforcement and the community to encourage cooperation from witnesses and victims.
   - Engage in community outreach and establish community policing practices to foster positive relationships.

10. Continuous Training and Professional Development:
   - Provide ongoing training and professional development opportunities for law enforcement and prosecutors to enhance their skills, knowledge, and understanding of evolving crime trends.

By addressing these obstacles and implementing strategies to overcome them, the criminal justice system can better serve the public, uphold the rule of law, and ensure that criminals are brought to justice. Collaboration between law enforcement, prosecutors, communities, and other stakeholders is crucial in navigating the challenges and fostering a more effective and accountable criminal justice system.

The impact of wrongful convictions and exonerations

Wrongful convictions and subsequent exonerations have significant and far-reaching impacts on individuals, families, the criminal justice system, and society as a whole. Some of the key effects include:

1. Miscarriage of Justice:
   - Wrongful convictions represent a miscarriage of justice, where innocent individuals are convicted and punished for crimes they did not commit. This undermines public trust in the fairness and reliability of the criminal justice system.
2. Personal and Psychological Trauma:
   - Wrongfully convicted individuals endure immense personal and psychological trauma, as they face the loss of freedom, separation from loved ones, and the stigma associated with being labeled as criminals.
3. Loss of Years or Decades of Life:
   - Exonerees may spend years or even decades behind bars for crimes they did not commit. Upon release, they must cope with the challenges of reintegration and rebuilding their lives.
4. Impact on Families:
   - Wrongful convictions affect the families of the accused, who may suffer emotionally,

financially, and socially due to the wrongful imprisonment of their loved ones.

5. Ineffectiveness of the Criminal Justice System:
   - Wrongful convictions expose flaws and weaknesses in the criminal justice system, including errors in investigations, flawed evidence, witness misidentification, and misconduct by law enforcement or prosecutors.

6. Cost to Society:
   - The process of exoneration, including investigations, legal proceedings, and compensation for the wrongfully convicted, can be financially burdensome to the state and taxpayers.

7. Impaired Public Confidence:
   - Wrongful convictions can erode public confidence in the criminal justice system, leading to skepticism about the reliability of convictions and the potential for more wrongful convictions to go undetected.

8. Identifying Systemic Problems:
   - Exonerations can shed light on systemic problems in the justice system, prompting reforms and policy changes to prevent similar errors in the future.

9. Reforms and Policy Changes:
   - High-profile cases of wrongful convictions have sparked discussions and calls for reforms, leading to changes in procedures related to eyewitness identification, forensic evidence analysis, and the use of informants, among other areas.

10. Compensation and Support:
    - After exoneration, some individuals receive compensation from the state, but this does not fully

restore the years lost or the damage done. Additionally, support services are often inadequate for exonerees attempting to rebuild their lives.

11. Impact on Victims and True Perpetrators:

. Wrongful convictions may divert resources and attention away from finding the true perpetrators, potentially delaying justice for the actual victims and hindering the resolution of cases.

Addressing and preventing wrongful convictions require ongoing efforts to improve investigative practices, enhance legal representation, bolster the use of forensic science, and ensure that justice is pursued fairly and transparently. Exonerations highlight the importance of continually striving for a criminal justice system that respects the rights of all individuals and guarantees justice for the innocent.

Technological Advancements and Criminal Law

Technological advancements have significantly impacted the field of criminal law, revolutionizing the way crimes are investigated, evidence is presented, and justice is served. These advancements have both positive and challenging implications for the criminal justice system. Here are some key ways in which technology has influenced criminal law:

1. Digital Evidence:
   - Digital evidence, such as data from computers, smartphones, social media, and surveillance cameras, has become crucial in many criminal investigations.
   - Technological tools enable the retrieval, analysis, and preservation of digital evidence, aiding law enforcement in solving crimes and presenting compelling evidence in court.
2. Forensic Technology:
   - Forensic technology has evolved to include advanced DNA analysis, fingerprint recognition, ballistic analysis, and other methods that help link suspects to crime scenes and exonerate innocent individuals.
   - These technologies enhance the accuracy and reliability of evidence, reducing the risk of wrongful convictions.
3. Surveillance and Monitoring:
   - The proliferation of surveillance cameras,

both public and private, has enhanced the ability to monitor criminal activity and identify suspects.

- However, concerns about privacy and the potential for abuse of surveillance technology have arisen, necessitating careful legal and ethical considerations.

4. Artificial Intelligence (AI):

- AI and machine learning algorithms can be applied to analyze vast amounts of data, aiding in predictive policing, crime pattern analysis, and criminal profiling.
- AI-powered technologies also have potential applications in legal research and case analysis, streamlining legal processes.

5. Cybercrime and Digital Security:

- Technology has given rise to new forms of criminal activity, such as cybercrime, hacking, and identity theft.
- Law enforcement agencies and legal systems must adapt to effectively combat these technologically sophisticated offenses.

6. E-Discovery and Digital Document Management:

- In legal proceedings, e-discovery has become essential for handling large volumes of digital documents and electronically stored information (ESI).
- Digital document management systems facilitate the organization and presentation of evidence during trials.

7. Cloud Computing and Data Storage:

- Cloud computing has transformed the way data is stored, accessed, and shared, impacting the management and protection of evidence in criminal cases.
- Ensuring data security and preventing

unauthorized access to sensitive information are critical concerns.

8. Communication and Cyberbullying:
   - The rise of digital communication platforms has given rise to cyberbullying and online harassment, leading to the need for updated legislation to address these offenses.

9. Automated Decision-Making and Bias:
   - The use of algorithms in pretrial risk assessment and sentencing decisions has raised concerns about potential bias and discrimination.
   - Ensuring fairness and transparency in algorithmic decision-making remains a challenge.

10. Virtual Courtrooms and Remote Proceedings:
   - Technological advancements have allowed for virtual courtrooms and remote proceedings, providing greater access to justice and reducing logistical challenges.

Embracing technological advancements in criminal law can enhance the efficiency and accuracy of the justice system. However, it also requires careful consideration of ethical, privacy, and constitutional issues to ensure that technology serves justice while protecting individual rights and civil liberties. Striking the right balance between innovation and safeguarding fundamental principles remains a critical aspect of navigating technology's impact on criminal law.

Digital evidence and challenges in preserving its integrity

Digital evidence plays a critical role in modern criminal investigations and court proceedings. It includes data stored on computers, smartphones, social media platforms, cloud services, surveillance cameras, and other electronic devices. Preserving the integrity of digital evidence is essential to ensure its admissibility and reliability in court. However, several challenges can arise in the process of preserving digital evidence:

1. Volatility: Digital evidence is highly volatile and can easily be altered, deleted, or overwritten if not properly handled. Actions such as powering off a device, connecting it to a network, or running certain programs can inadvertently modify or erase evidence.

2. Encryption and Password Protection: Encrypted data and password-protected devices present challenges for investigators trying to access and preserve evidence. Without the proper decryption keys or passwords, investigators may face difficulty in accessing critical information.

3. Data Encryption in Transit: Data transmitted over the internet may be encrypted, making it difficult to intercept and preserve as evidence during transmission.

4. Time Sensitivity: Digital evidence can be time-sensitive, particularly in cybercrime cases or instances where data may be deleted or altered quickly.

Investigators must act swiftly to secure evidence before it is lost or changed.

5. Chain of Custody: Maintaining a secure chain of custody for digital evidence is crucial to establish its authenticity and reliability in court. Mishandling or improper documentation of evidence transfers can compromise its integrity.

6. Data Volume: The sheer volume of digital evidence collected in modern investigations can be overwhelming. Investigators need efficient tools and processes to collect, store, and manage large amounts of data.

7. Data Compression: Some digital evidence, such as images and videos, may be compressed to save storage space. Compression can affect the quality and integrity of the data.

8. Data Fragmentation: Data stored on electronic devices may be fragmented, scattered across different storage locations. Properly reconstructing and preserving fragmented data can be challenging.

9. Anti-Forensic Techniques: Criminals may use anti-forensic techniques to hide or destroy digital evidence, making it harder for investigators to retrieve and preserve the information.

10. Remote Storage and Cloud Services: Digital evidence stored remotely or on cloud services may require legal processes, cooperation with service providers, and data retrieval mechanisms to ensure its preservation.

To address these challenges and preserve the integrity of digital evidence, investigators and legal professionals use specialized tools and techniques, such as write-blocking devices, digital forensic software, and secure storage systems. Additionally, adherence to proper procedures, documentation, and expert testimony during court proceedings helps establish the credibility and authenticity of digital evidence. As technology continues to evolve, staying abreast of best practices and advancements in digital forensics is crucial in maintaining the integrity of digital evidence in criminal investigations.

The use of technology in crime detection and prevention

The use of technology in crime detection and prevention has revolutionized law enforcement practices, enhancing the ability to identify, track, and apprehend criminals, as well as preventing criminal activities. Here are some key ways technology is utilized for crime detection and prevention:

1. Surveillance Systems: Advanced surveillance cameras and CCTV systems are strategically placed in public areas, transportation hubs, and critical infrastructures to monitor activities and deter potential criminals. These systems also aid in identifying suspects and gathering evidence after a crime has occurred.

2. Predictive Policing: Technology enables the use of data analytics and machine learning algorithms to identify crime hotspots and patterns, allowing law enforcement agencies to allocate resources more efficiently and proactively prevent criminal activities.

3. Digital Forensics: Digital forensics tools and techniques help investigators retrieve, analyze, and preserve digital evidence from computers, smartphones, and other electronic devices, aiding in solving cybercrimes and traditional crimes involving digital evidence.

4. DNA Analysis: Advancements in DNA analysis technology have revolutionized criminal investigations by providing accurate identification and linking suspects to crime scenes, leading to more

successful prosecutions and exonerations.

5. Biometric Identification: Biometric technologies such as fingerprint, facial recognition, and iris scanning are used to identify individuals, helping in locating suspects and preventing unauthorized access to sensitive areas.

6. Cybersecurity Measures: Cybersecurity tools and protocols are employed to protect critical infrastructure, government networks, and private businesses from cyberattacks and data breaches.

7. GPS Tracking: Global Positioning System (GPS) technology is used to track the movement of vehicles and devices, aiding in locating stolen property, monitoring parolees, and investigating criminal activities.

8. Social Media and Open Source Intelligence (OSINT): Law enforcement agencies use social media and OSINT to gather information about individuals and potential criminal activities, supporting investigations and intelligence gathering.

9. Mobile Apps for Reporting: Mobile applications allow the public to report crimes, suspicious activities, and emergencies quickly, facilitating community engagement in crime prevention efforts.

10. Automated License Plate Recognition (ALPR): ALPR technology scans license plates and matches them against databases of stolen vehicles or vehicles associated with criminal activities, helping law enforcement identify suspect vehicles.

11. Drones and Robotics: Drones and robots equipped with cameras and sensors can access hard-to-reach areas, providing real-time surveillance and assisting in search and rescue operations.

12. Crime Analysis Software: Crime analysis software helps law enforcement agencies analyze crime data, identify trends, and make informed decisions to

improve crime prevention strategies.

While technology offers significant benefits in crime detection and prevention, its use raises ethical and privacy concerns. Striking the right balance between effective crime-fighting tools and safeguarding civil liberties is crucial for the responsible implementation of technology in law enforcement practices. Additionally, continuous training and updating of technology for law enforcement personnel are essential to ensure effective and responsible use of these tools in the fight against crime.

Balancing privacy rights and law enforcement in the digital age

Balancing privacy rights and law enforcement in the digital age is a complex and multifaceted challenge. On one hand, protecting individual privacy is a fundamental right and a cornerstone of democratic societies. On the other hand, law enforcement agencies need access to information and data to investigate and prevent crimes effectively. Striking the right balance between these two interests requires careful consideration and thoughtful approaches. Here are some key considerations for achieving this balance:

1. Clear Legal Frameworks: Establish clear and comprehensive legal frameworks that define the scope and limitations of law enforcement's access to digital data and information. Laws should be regularly reviewed and updated to keep pace with technological advancements and evolving privacy concerns.

2. Warrants and Probable Cause: Require law enforcement to obtain warrants based on probable cause before accessing private digital information or conducting electronic surveillance. This ensures judicial oversight and protects against arbitrary invasions of privacy.

3. Data Minimization: Encourage data minimization practices, where law enforcement agencies only collect and retain the minimum amount of data necessary for specific investigations. This reduces the risk of unnecessary intrusion into individuals' private lives.

4. Encryption and Data Security: Encourage the use of strong encryption and data security measures to protect individuals' data from unauthorized access and cyber threats. Striking a balance between encryption and lawful access is essential.

5. Transparency and Accountability: Foster transparency in law enforcement practices and promote accountability. Public reporting on the use of surveillance technologies and data collection can help build public trust and confidence.

6. Independent Oversight: Establish independent oversight bodies to review and monitor law enforcement's use of digital technologies and ensure compliance with privacy laws and regulations.

7. Technology Neutrality: Ensure that privacy protections apply regardless of the technology used. Whether information is stored physically or in the cloud, the same privacy standards should be upheld.

8. Data Retention Policies: Implement clear data retention policies that specify the duration for which law enforcement can retain collected data. Unnecessary retention increases the risk of privacy breaches.

9. Judicial Review: Enable individuals to challenge law enforcement actions in court if they believe their privacy rights have been violated. Independent judicial review provides a check on law enforcement's powers.

10. International Cooperation: Promote international cooperation and agreements on privacy and data protection to address cross-border challenges posed by digital data and investigations.

11. Training and Education: Provide ongoing training for law enforcement personnel on privacy laws, ethical considerations, and best practices in digital investigations.

12. Public Dialogue: Encourage open and inclusive public

dialogue about the balance between privacy rights and law enforcement needs. Engaging the public and stakeholders can lead to better policy outcomes.

Balancing privacy rights and law enforcement in the digital age is an ongoing process that requires collaboration among policymakers, law enforcement agencies, technologists, privacy advocates, and the public. By incorporating these considerations into legal frameworks and practices, societies can safeguard individual privacy while maintaining effective law enforcement capabilities.

Alternatives to Traditional Criminal Justice

In recent years, alternatives to traditional criminal justice systems have gained traction as more people recognize the need for innovative approaches to address crime and promote rehabilitation. These alternatives aim to reduce recidivism, promote restorative justice, and address systemic issues within the criminal justice system. Some notable alternatives include:

1. Restorative Justice: Restorative justice focuses on repairing the harm caused by crimes through dialogue and reconciliation between victims, offenders, and the community. It seeks to hold offenders accountable while addressing the needs of victims and promoting healing and restoration.

2. Diversion Programs: Diversion programs offer eligible offenders an opportunity to avoid formal prosecution by participating in rehabilitation or treatment programs. These programs aim to address the root causes of criminal behavior and prevent further involvement in the criminal justice system.

3. Drug Courts: Drug courts are specialized courts that focus on the treatment and rehabilitation of individuals with substance abuse issues. Participants are given the opportunity to undergo treatment and counseling instead of traditional sentencing.

4. Mental Health Courts: Mental health courts provide specialized services and treatment for individuals with mental health issues involved in the criminal

justice system. The goal is to address underlying mental health issues and reduce the likelihood of reoffending.

5. Community-Based Sentencing: Community-based sentencing involves sentencing offenders to serve their sentences in the community under supervision, such as probation or community service. This approach allows individuals to remain connected to their support networks and access necessary services.

6. Pretrial Diversion: Pretrial diversion programs divert individuals charged with minor offenses away from traditional court proceedings. Participants may be required to attend counseling, perform community service, or participate in educational programs.

7. Community Policing: Community policing emphasizes collaboration between law enforcement and the community to address local crime issues. By building trust and engaging with residents, community policing seeks to prevent crime through proactive efforts.

8. Mediation and Conflict Resolution: Mediation and conflict resolution programs help resolve disputes between individuals, including some criminal cases, without going through traditional court processes.

9. Holistic Defense: Holistic defense involves providing legal representation while also addressing clients' social and economic needs, such as housing, employment, and healthcare. This comprehensive approach aims to address the root causes of criminal behavior.

10. Decriminalization: Decriminalization involves reducing or eliminating criminal penalties for certain offenses, focusing on alternative responses, such as civil citations or fines.

11. Peacemaking Circles: Peacemaking circles are Indigenous and traditional practices that bring

together individuals impacted by a crime to discuss the harm caused and seek solutions collaboratively.

By exploring and implementing these alternatives, communities can work towards a more just and effective criminal justice system that prioritizes rehabilitation, prevention, and restorative approaches to crime. These alternatives recognize that punishment alone may not lead to lasting positive change and that addressing the underlying issues that contribute to criminal behavior is essential for building safer and more resilient communities.

Diversion programs and community-based sentencing

Diversion programs and community-based sentencing are two alternative approaches to traditional criminal justice that aim to address the root causes of criminal behavior and reduce recidivism. Both approaches focus on rehabilitation, treatment, and community involvement as opposed to punitive measures. Let's explore each of these alternatives in more detail:

1. Diversion Programs: Diversion programs offer eligible individuals charged with minor offenses an alternative to traditional prosecution. Instead of going through the regular criminal court process, participants are diverted to specialized programs or interventions tailored to their specific needs. These programs aim to address the underlying issues that may have contributed to the individual's involvement in the criminal justice system, such as substance abuse, mental health issues, or socioeconomic challenges. Common types of diversion programs include:

a. Pretrial Diversion: Allows individuals to avoid formal prosecution by completing certain requirements, such as counseling, community service, or educational programs.

b. Drug Diversion: Focuses on providing treatment and counseling to individuals with substance abuse issues rather than incarceration.

c. Mental Health Diversion: Provides specialized services and treatment for individuals with mental health conditions who have committed non-violent offenses.

d. Juvenile Diversion: Diversion programs designed for youth offenders to prevent their involvement in the juvenile justice system.

Diversion programs offer several benefits, including reduced recidivism rates, cost-effectiveness, and a focus on rehabilitation and addressing the underlying causes of criminal behavior.

2. Community-Based Sentencing: Community-based sentencing involves sentencing offenders to serve their sentences in the community under supervision, rather than in jail or prison. It emphasizes rehabilitation and reintegration while allowing individuals to remain connected to their support networks. Community-based sentences can include:

a. Probation: Offenders are released into the community under certain conditions and supervision, such as regular check-ins with a probation officer and adherence to specific rules.

b. Community Service: Offenders perform unpaid work within the community as a form of restitution and contribution to society.

c. Restitution: Offenders are required to compensate victims for any financial losses or damages resulting from their crimes.

d. Home Confinement or Electronic Monitoring: Offenders are confined to their homes or monitored electronically to ensure compliance with their sentence.

Community-based sentencing aims to promote accountability while providing opportunities for rehabilitation and personal growth. It allows offenders to maintain employment, support their families, and access necessary services that can contribute to successful reintegration into society.

By diverting individuals from traditional court processes and providing community-based alternatives, diversion programs and community-based sentencing seek to break the cycle of crime by addressing underlying issues and fostering a sense of responsibility and connection to the community. These approaches can lead to positive outcomes for both individuals and society, promoting safer communities and reducing the strain on the criminal justice system.

Problem-solving courts (e.g., drug courts, mental health courts)

Problem-solving courts, also known as specialized or treatment courts, are a type of alternative court model that focuses on addressing the underlying issues that contribute to criminal behavior. These courts seek to promote rehabilitation, reduce recidivism, and improve outcomes for individuals facing specific challenges, such as substance abuse or mental health issues. Problem-solving courts operate under a collaborative and interdisciplinary approach, involving judges, prosecutors, defense attorneys, treatment providers, and community stakeholders. Some common types of problem-solving courts include:

1. Drug Courts: Drug courts are specialized courts designed to handle cases involving individuals with substance abuse or addiction issues. Instead of traditional punitive measures, drug courts offer a combination of treatment, counseling, and judicial oversight. Participants are required to complete a substance abuse treatment program and adhere to strict monitoring and drug testing protocols. Successful completion of the program may result in reduced charges or dismissal of charges.

2. Mental Health Courts: Mental health courts are dedicated to addressing cases involving individuals with mental health conditions who have committed non-violent offenses. These courts aim to connect participants with appropriate mental health services

and treatment, rather than incarcerating them. Participants must comply with treatment plans and engage in supportive services as part of their court-supervised program.

3. Veterans Courts: Veterans courts are specialized courts that cater to veterans who are involved in the criminal justice system. They focus on addressing underlying issues related to military service, such as post-traumatic stress disorder (PTSD) or substance abuse, by providing targeted treatment and support.

4. Homeless Courts: Homeless courts are designed for individuals experiencing homelessness who have committed minor offenses related to their housing situation. These courts aim to address homelessness through supportive services, housing assistance, and community-based solutions.

5. DUI Courts: DUI courts, also known as DWI courts, focus on repeat DUI (driving under the influence) offenders. The courts offer intensive treatment, education, and monitoring to address the underlying issues contributing to repeat DUI offenses.

The key features and benefits of problem-solving courts include:

- Tailored Interventions: Problem-solving courts provide individualized treatment plans based on the specific needs of participants, taking into account the factors contributing to their criminal behavior.
- Judicial Oversight: Judges in problem-solving courts actively engage with participants, monitoring their progress, and providing guidance and support throughout the program.
- Collaborative Approach: These courts involve a range of professionals, including judges, prosecutors, defense attorneys, treatment providers, and social workers, to create a comprehensive and coordinated

approach to rehabilitation.

- Reduced Recidivism: Studies have shown that problem-solving courts can lead to lower recidivism rates compared to traditional court processes, as they address the root causes of criminal behavior.

Problem-solving courts have demonstrated promising results in diverting individuals from the traditional criminal justice system, reducing recidivism rates, and promoting rehabilitation and community reintegration. They play a vital role in addressing the complexities of certain offenses and the unique challenges faced by participants, aiming to break the cycle of criminal behavior and improve outcomes for both individuals and society.

The role of restorative justice
in resolving conflicts

Restorative justice is a unique and transformative approach to resolving conflicts and addressing harm caused by criminal behavior. Unlike punitive approaches that focus on punishing offenders, restorative justice emphasizes repairing the harm done to victims, holding offenders accountable, and promoting healing within the affected community. It aims to bring all parties involved in a crime together to participate in a facilitated dialogue, allowing them to address the impact of the offense, find resolution, and work towards reconciliation. The key principles and roles of restorative justice in conflict resolution are as follows:

1. Victim-Centered Approach: Restorative justice places the needs and experiences of victims at the forefront of the process. It gives victims the opportunity to share their feelings, ask questions, and express their needs for healing and closure.

2. Accountability and Responsibility: Offenders are encouraged to take responsibility for their actions and understand the harm caused to victims and the community. This accountability fosters a sense of personal growth and ownership over their actions.

3. Dialogue and Communication: Restorative justice creates a safe and respectful space for dialogue between victims and offenders, allowing them to communicate directly and openly about the impact of the offense and its consequences.

4. Reconciliation and Healing: The primary goal of restorative justice is to promote healing and reconciliation for all parties involved. It seeks to repair the broken relationships between victims, offenders, and the community, fostering a sense of closure and restoration.

5. Community Involvement: Restorative justice involves the wider community in the resolution process. Community members, including family, friends, and other stakeholders, can participate in the dialogue and offer support.

6. Voluntary Participation: Participation in restorative justice processes is voluntary, meaning that victims and offenders can choose to engage or not. However, the opportunity to participate can be offered to those willing to engage in the process.

7. Facilitator Role: A trained facilitator guides the restorative justice process, ensuring that communication is respectful and focused on addressing the harm caused rather than assigning blame.

8. Agreement and Follow-Through: In many cases, agreements are reached during the restorative justice process. These agreements outline the steps for making amends, repairing harm, and addressing the needs of all parties involved. Follow-through on these agreements is critical to building trust and ensuring that the process is meaningful and effective.

Restorative justice offers a powerful alternative to the traditional criminal justice system by providing a way for victims, offenders, and the community to come together and actively participate in the resolution of conflicts. By promoting empathy, understanding, and collaboration, restorative justice fosters healing and transformation, allowing all parties to move forward with a greater sense of closure and accountability. It not only addresses the immediate harm caused by the offense but also contributes to the prevention of future conflicts and crimes by addressing the root causes of criminal behavior.

Criminal Law and Human Rights

Criminal law and human rights are intricately linked, as criminal justice systems play a critical role in upholding and protecting human rights. The relationship between criminal law and human rights can be seen in several key aspects:

1. Protection of Individual Rights: Criminal law is designed to protect the rights of individuals from harm and violation by defining and punishing criminal behavior. Laws against offenses such as assault, theft, and murder are essential for safeguarding the right to life, bodily integrity, and property.

2. Right to a Fair Trial: Human rights principles, including the right to a fair trial, are fundamental in criminal proceedings. This includes the right to legal representation, the presumption of innocence, access to evidence, the right to remain silent, and protection against self-incrimination.

3. Prohibition of Torture and Cruel Punishment: Human rights law strictly prohibits torture and cruel, inhuman, or degrading treatment or punishment. Criminal law ensures that these principles are enforced and that perpetrators of such acts are held accountable.

4. Right to Privacy: Criminal law is connected to the right to privacy, as laws against illegal searches and seizures protect individuals from unwarranted intrusion into their private lives by law enforcement agencies.

5. Freedom of Expression: Criminal law must balance

the right to freedom of expression with the need to address hate speech, incitement to violence, and other forms of harmful speech that can lead to criminal acts.

6. Protection of Vulnerable Populations: Criminal law plays a vital role in protecting vulnerable populations, including children, women, minorities, and marginalized groups, from discrimination, violence, and exploitation.

7. Right to Access Justice and Redress: Criminal law ensures that victims of crimes have the right to access justice and seek redress for the harm they have suffered.

8. Accountability for Human Rights Violations: Criminal law provides a framework for holding individuals and entities accountable for human rights violations, including crimes against humanity, genocide, and war crimes.

9. Limitations on Criminalization: Human rights principles impose limitations on the scope of criminal law to prevent arbitrary and discriminatory criminalization, protecting individuals from unjust and oppressive laws.

10. Non-Discrimination: Criminal law should be applied without discrimination, ensuring equal protection under the law for all individuals, regardless of race, religion, gender, or other protected characteristics.

However, it is crucial to note that the criminal justice system is not immune to human rights challenges. Issues such as racial profiling, excessive use of force by law enforcement, overcrowded prisons, and the use of the death penalty in some countries raise concerns about potential human rights violations within criminal justice systems.

Striking the right balance between upholding human rights and effectively addressing crime is a continuous challenge for legal systems worldwide. Policymakers, legal professionals, and society as a whole must remain vigilant in promoting human rights principles within criminal law and ensuring that the criminal justice system operates in a fair, just, and rights-respecting manner.

Protecting individual rights in criminal proceedings

Protecting individual rights in criminal proceedings is a fundamental principle of the rule of law and a cornerstone of a fair and just criminal justice system. Several key rights are enshrined in international human rights instruments and national legal systems to ensure that individuals accused of crimes are treated fairly and that their rights are upheld throughout the criminal process. Some of the most essential rights include:

1. Right to a Fair Trial: The right to a fair trial is a fundamental human right guaranteed by international human rights treaties, such as the Universal Declaration of Human Rights and the International Covenant on Civil and Political Rights (ICCPR). It includes the right to be heard by an impartial and competent tribunal, the right to legal representation, the right to call and examine witnesses, and the right to access evidence.

2. Presumption of Innocence: The presumption of innocence is a core principle in criminal law, stating that an accused person is considered innocent until proven guilty beyond a reasonable doubt. This principle protects individuals from being treated as guilty before their guilt is established in a court of law.

3. Right to Legal Counsel: The right to legal counsel ensures that individuals accused of crimes have access to legal representation throughout the criminal

proceedings. This right helps to balance the inherent power imbalance between the accused and the state.

4. Right to Remain Silent: The right to remain silent protects individuals from being compelled to self-incriminate. It means that an accused person has the right not to answer questions posed by law enforcement or other authorities during the investigation or trial.

5. Right to be Informed of Charges: Accused individuals have the right to be informed of the charges against them in a language they understand. This right is essential to enable individuals to prepare their defense adequately.

6. Right to a Speedy Trial: The right to a speedy trial ensures that accused individuals are not subjected to lengthy pretrial detention or delays in resolving their cases.

7. Right to Confront Witnesses: The right to confront witnesses allows accused individuals to cross-examine witnesses presented by the prosecution, challenging their testimony and credibility.

8. Right to Habeas Corpus: The right to habeas corpus protects individuals from unlawful detention, allowing them to challenge the legality of their detention before a court.

9. Right to Protection from Double Jeopardy: The principle of double jeopardy prohibits individuals from being tried or punished twice for the same offense, protecting them from multiple prosecutions for the same crime.

10. Right to Appeal: The right to appeal ensures that accused individuals have the opportunity to challenge the verdict or sentence handed down in their cases.

11. Right to Due Process: The right to due process ensures that individuals are provided with a fair and transparent process in criminal proceedings,

including adequate notice, an opportunity to be heard, and a neutral decision-maker.

Respecting and upholding these individual rights is essential to ensure that the criminal justice system operates fairly and effectively. Legal professionals, law enforcement agencies, and judicial authorities play a vital role in safeguarding these rights and ensuring that accused individuals are treated with dignity, respect, and fairness throughout the criminal process.

The prohibition of torture and cruel, inhuman, or degrading treatment

The prohibition of torture and cruel, inhuman, or degrading treatment is a fundamental principle of international human rights law. It is enshrined in various international treaties and conventions, including the Universal Declaration of Human Rights, the International Covenant on Civil and Political Rights (ICCPR), and the Convention against Torture and Other Cruel, Inhuman or Degrading Treatment or Punishment (CAT).

The prohibition serves as a powerful protection against the use of violence, coercion, or mistreatment by state actors or non-state actors against individuals in any circumstances. Key aspects of this prohibition include:

1. Definition of Torture: The Convention against Torture defines torture as any act by which severe pain or suffering, whether physical or mental, is intentionally inflicted on a person for purposes such as obtaining information, punishment, intimidation, or discrimination.

2. Non-derogable Right: The prohibition of torture and cruel, inhuman, or degrading treatment is considered a non-derogable right, meaning that it cannot be suspended or waived even in times of emergency or conflict.

3. Absolute Nature: The prohibition is absolute and unconditional, leaving no room for exceptions or justifications. No circumstance, including war or

threat to national security, can justify the use of torture or cruel treatment.

4. State Responsibility: States are responsible for ensuring that torture and cruel treatment are not practiced within their territories or by their officials. This responsibility includes prevention, investigation, prosecution, and redress for victims.

5. Extraterritorial Application: The prohibition of torture applies not only within a state's territory but also to its agents and officials operating outside its borders, including in situations of armed conflict or peacekeeping operations.

6. No Extradition to Torture: The principle of non-refoulement prohibits the extradition or deportation of individuals to countries where they may face a risk of torture.

7. International Monitoring: International bodies, such as the United Nations Committee against Torture, monitor states' compliance with their obligations under the CAT and provide recommendations to enhance protection against torture.

The prohibition of torture and cruel treatment is considered a jus cogens norm, a peremptory norm of international law that enjoys a special status and is binding on all states. It reflects a global consensus on the absolute and inviolable nature of this human rights norm.

Despite the clear international legal framework, torture and cruel treatment continue to occur in some parts of the world, often in secretive settings and without accountability. Efforts to combat torture include raising awareness, strengthening the capacity of legal systems, promoting preventive measures, and holding perpetrators accountable through impartial and fair trials.

Overall, the prohibition of torture and cruel, inhuman,

or degrading treatment is a cornerstone of human rights protection, reflecting humanity's commitment to respecting the dignity and inherent worth of every individual. Upholding this prohibition is essential for building societies based on justice, respect for human rights, and the rule of law.

The right to a fair trial and due process

The right to a fair trial and due process are fundamental human rights that form the bedrock of a just and equitable legal system. These rights are enshrined in international human rights instruments, such as the Universal Declaration of Human Rights and the International Covenant on Civil and Political Rights (ICCPR), as well as in many national constitutions and legal systems worldwide. The right to a fair trial and due process ensures that individuals facing legal proceedings are accorded essential safeguards and protections, regardless of their guilt or innocence.

Key components of the right to a fair trial and due process include:

1. Presumption of Innocence: The principle of the presumption of innocence holds that every person accused of a crime is considered innocent until proven guilty beyond a reasonable doubt. This means that the burden of proving guilt rests with the prosecution, and the accused is not required to prove their innocence.

2. Impartial and Competent Tribunal: The right to a fair trial guarantees that the case is heard by an impartial and competent tribunal, free from any bias or influence that could affect the proceedings' fairness.

3. Right to Legal Counsel: Accused individuals have the right to be represented by legal counsel throughout the entire legal process, from the investigation stage to the trial and appeals, ensuring that they can present a robust defense and navigate the complexities of the legal system.

4. Right to Be Informed of Charges: The accused has the right to be informed promptly and in detail of the nature and cause of the charges against them. This ensures that they are aware of the allegations and can prepare an adequate defense.

5. Right to a Public Trial: The right to a public trial allows trials to be conducted in open court, promoting transparency and accountability in the justice system. However, certain circumstances, such as national security concerns or protecting the privacy of the parties involved, may warrant closed proceedings.

6. Right to Confront Witnesses: Accused individuals have the right to cross-examine witnesses presented by the prosecution, allowing them to challenge the credibility and accuracy of the evidence against them.

7. Right to Remain Silent: The right to remain silent protects accused individuals from being compelled to incriminate themselves. They have the right not to testify or provide evidence against themselves.

8. Right to Present Evidence: Accused individuals have the right to present evidence in their favor and call witnesses to support their defense.

9. Right to a Speedy Trial: The right to a speedy trial ensures that accused individuals are not subject to undue delays in the legal process, protecting them from prolonged pretrial detention.

10. Right to Appellate Review: The right to appellate review allows accused individuals to challenge the trial court's decision before a higher court if they believe that errors were made during the trial.

11. Right to Due Process: Due process requires that the accused be treated fairly and with respect for their legal rights throughout the entire legal process.

12. Right to an Interpreter: If the accused does not understand the language used in the court proceedings, they have the right to the assistance of an

interpreter.

The right to a fair trial and due process ensures that individuals accused of crimes are treated with dignity, fairness, and respect for their human rights. Upholding these rights is essential to prevent miscarriages of justice, protect innocent individuals from wrongful convictions, and maintain public trust in the legal system. The guarantee of a fair trial and due process is a fundamental aspect of the rule of law and the protection of human rights around the world.

Global Perspectives on Criminal Law

Global perspectives on criminal law refer to the diverse approaches, principles, and practices of criminal justice systems around the world. While criminal law is rooted in fundamental principles such as the protection of society and the administration of justice, its application can vary significantly from one jurisdiction to another due to cultural, historical, political, and legal differences. Understanding these global perspectives is crucial for fostering cooperation, promoting human rights, and addressing transnational crime effectively.

Some key aspects of global perspectives on criminal law include:

1. Legal Systems: The world's legal systems can be broadly categorized into common law, civil law, Islamic law, customary law, and religious law traditions. Each system influences how crimes are defined, prosecuted, and punished.

2. Criminalization: Different societies may criminalize certain behaviors differently, reflecting their cultural norms, values, and priorities. For instance, certain countries may decriminalize or adopt lenient measures for offenses considered serious in other jurisdictions.

3. Punishment and Rehabilitation: Approaches to punishment and rehabilitation can vary widely. Some countries emphasize retribution and deterrence, while others prioritize restorative justice and rehabilitation to address the root causes of criminal behavior.

4. Death Penalty: The use of the death penalty varies globally, with some countries retaining it for certain

offenses, while others have abolished it in favor of life imprisonment or other penalties.

5. Drug Policy: Drug laws and policies diverge across countries, ranging from strict prohibition to decriminalization or legalization of certain substances.

6. Juvenile Justice: The treatment of juvenile offenders varies significantly, with some jurisdictions emphasizing rehabilitation and diversion programs, while others adopt harsher measures.

7. Human Rights Protections: Global perspectives on criminal law are shaped by adherence to international human rights norms, such as the prohibition of torture, right to a fair trial, and protection of vulnerable populations.

8. Transnational Crime: Crimes that cross borders, such as terrorism, human trafficking, cybercrime, and drug trafficking, require international cooperation and coordination to combat effectively.

9. International Criminal Law: International criminal law addresses crimes of universal concern, such as genocide, war crimes, and crimes against humanity, through international tribunals and courts.

10. Cultural Sensitivity: Legal systems must be culturally sensitive to respect diverse norms and traditions while upholding human rights standards.

11. Legal Harmonization: Globalization has led to efforts to harmonize criminal laws across countries, particularly in areas such as cybercrime, terrorism, and corruption.

12. Restorative Justice: Restorative justice practices have gained traction globally as a means to address crime and promote reconciliation.

13. Law Enforcement Cooperation: Global perspectives on criminal law necessitate cooperation between law enforcement agencies across borders to investigate

and prosecute transnational crime.

Understanding global perspectives on criminal law allows for the exchange of best practices, mutual learning, and enhanced collaboration in combating crime and promoting human rights. It also underscores the importance of international law and cooperation in addressing the increasingly interconnected challenges faced by societies worldwide.

Comparative analysis of criminal justice systems in different countries

A comparative analysis of criminal justice systems in different countries involves examining and contrasting various aspects of how each system operates, including laws, procedures, institutions, and outcomes. Such analysis provides valuable insights into the strengths and weaknesses of each system and highlights potential areas for improvement. Here are some key aspects that can be compared:

1. Legal Framework: Compare the criminal laws of different countries, including definitions of crimes, elements of offenses, and penalties. Analyze how countries categorize crimes (e.g., felonies, misdemeanors) and the thresholds for each category.

2. Adversarial vs. Inquisitorial Systems: Compare countries with adversarial systems (e.g., common law countries like the United States) to those with inquisitorial systems (e.g., civil law countries like France). Examine how cases are investigated, prosecuted, and adjudicated under each system.

3. Role of Police: Compare the role of law enforcement agencies, their powers, and responsibilities in different countries. Analyze the mechanisms for oversight and accountability.

4. Legal Representation: Compare how legal representation is provided to accused individuals, including the availability of public defenders, legal aid, and the right to counsel.

5. Pretrial Detention: Analyze how countries handle pretrial detention and its duration, including bail systems and conditions for release.

6. Trial Procedures: Compare trial procedures, including the presentation of evidence, rules of evidence, the right to confront witnesses, and the use of juries.

7. Rights of the Accused: Examine the protection of rights such as the right to remain silent, the right to be informed of charges, and the right to a speedy trial.

8. Sentencing and Punishment: Compare sentencing practices, including the types of penalties imposed for different offenses and the availability of alternative sentencing options.

9. Juvenile Justice: Analyze how each country treats juvenile offenders and the measures in place for their rehabilitation and reintegration into society.

10. Human Rights Protections: Evaluate how each system upholds human rights, including protections against torture, cruel, inhuman, or degrading treatment, and discrimination.

11. Use of Technology: Examine the use of technology in criminal justice systems, such as electronic monitoring, digital evidence collection, and automated case management.

12. Rehabilitation and Reintegration: Compare efforts to rehabilitate offenders and facilitate their reintegration into society post-release.

13. Prison Conditions: Analyze the conditions and treatment of inmates in prisons, including efforts to address overcrowding and promote prisoner rehabilitation.

14. Restorative Justice Practices: Compare the adoption and implementation of restorative justice practices in different countries.

15. Access to Justice: Evaluate the accessibility of the criminal justice system to all segments of society,

including marginalized and vulnerable populations.

16. International Cooperation: Analyze the level of international cooperation in tackling transnational crime and extradition arrangements.

A comprehensive comparative analysis of criminal justice systems can provide valuable insights into best practices, challenges, and areas of improvement for countries seeking to enhance their legal systems' fairness, efficiency, and adherence to human rights principles. It also promotes cross-border learning and cooperation to address common global challenges in crime and justice.

International criminal law and efforts to address transnational crimes

International criminal law is a branch of law that deals with crimes of international concern and seeks to hold individuals accountable for committing such crimes. It focuses on offenses that have significant international implications, transcend national borders, and harm the global community. Efforts to address transnational crimes through international criminal law involve several key aspects:

1. International Criminal Tribunals: International criminal tribunals, such as the International Criminal Court (ICC), are established to prosecute individuals accused of committing serious crimes under international law. These crimes include genocide, war crimes, crimes against humanity, and the crime of aggression.

2. Universal Jurisdiction: Universal jurisdiction allows national courts to prosecute individuals for certain international crimes, regardless of where the crime was committed or the nationality of the accused or the victims. This ensures that those responsible for grave offenses do not find safe havens.

3. Extradition: Extradition treaties and mechanisms facilitate the transfer of suspects or accused individuals from one country to another to face prosecution for transnational crimes.

4. Mutual Legal Assistance: Countries cooperate through mutual legal assistance treaties to share evidence,

witness testimony, and other relevant information for the investigation and prosecution of transnational crimes.

5. International Cooperation: International cooperation among law enforcement agencies helps track and apprehend criminals who cross borders to evade justice.

6. Suppression of Terrorist Financing: Countries work together to prevent the flow of funds to terrorist organizations and disrupt their financial networks.

7. Combating Cybercrime: International efforts address cybercrimes that target individuals, businesses, or governments in multiple countries.

8. Combatting Human Trafficking: International efforts combat human trafficking, which involves the illegal movement of people across borders for exploitation.

9. Addressing Drug Trafficking: International cooperation targets drug trafficking networks that operate across multiple jurisdictions.

10. Combating Money Laundering: International initiatives address money laundering that facilitates transnational crimes.

11. Addressing Environmental Crimes: International cooperation is essential to address transnational environmental crimes, such as illegal wildlife trade and illegal logging.

12. Accountability for International Crimes: International criminal law plays a crucial role in holding individuals accountable for atrocities committed during armed conflicts, such as genocide, war crimes, and crimes against humanity.

13. Promoting Human Rights: International criminal law contributes to the promotion and protection of human rights by prosecuting those responsible for gross human rights violations.

14. Restorative Justice: In some cases, international

criminal law incorporates restorative justice principles to address the needs of victims and affected communities.

Efforts to address transnational crimes through international criminal law face challenges, including issues of jurisdiction, extradition complexities, and limitations in enforcing international arrest warrants. However, the growing recognition of the need for global cooperation in combating these crimes demonstrates the importance of international criminal law in promoting accountability and upholding the rule of law on a global scale.

Challenges in extradition and international cooperation in criminal matters

Extradition and international cooperation in criminal matters are essential for addressing transnational crime and ensuring that individuals accused of committing crimes are brought to justice. However, several challenges hinder effective cooperation between countries:

1. Legal and Political Barriers: Extradition is governed by bilateral or multilateral treaties, and the existence of such treaties between countries may vary. In the absence of a relevant treaty, countries may face legal obstacles to extradite suspects.

2. Dual Criminality: Many extradition treaties require that the offense for which extradition is sought must be a crime in both the requesting and requested countries. If the offense is not recognized as a crime in the requested country, extradition may be denied.

3. Political Considerations: Extradition may become politically sensitive, especially in high-profile cases or when the requesting country's legal system is perceived as unfair or politically motivated.

4. Human Rights Concerns: Extradition requests may be denied if there are concerns about the suspect's human rights being violated in the requesting country, such as the possibility of facing torture or an unfair trial.

5. Death Penalty: Some countries refuse to extradite suspects to jurisdictions where they may face the death penalty, unless assurances are given that the

death penalty will not be imposed.

6. Complexity of Transnational Investigations: Cooperation in complex investigations involving multiple jurisdictions requires coordination, mutual legal assistance, and the exchange of evidence, which can be time-consuming and challenging.

7. Lack of Capacity and Resources: Some countries may lack the capacity or resources to effectively investigate transnational crimes or provide assistance in foreign criminal matters.

8. Jurisdictional Challenges: Determining which country has jurisdiction over a particular crime can be challenging when offenses involve actors or conduct across multiple borders.

9. Language and Cultural Barriers: Differences in language, legal systems, and cultural practices can complicate cooperation and communication between countries.

10. Asymmetry of Extradition Treaties: Some extradition treaties may be asymmetrical, favoring one country over the other, leading to potential tensions and reluctance to cooperate fully.

11. Non-Cooperative Jurisdictions: Some countries may be non-cooperative or refuse to cooperate in certain cases, hindering efforts to bring offenders to justice.

12. Fugitives in Safe Havens: Some suspects may find refuge in countries with weak extradition laws or without extradition treaties, making it difficult to apprehend and prosecute them.

To address these challenges, countries must work together to strengthen international cooperation mechanisms, promote the rule of law, and respect human rights standards. Regional and international organizations play a crucial role in facilitating cooperation, harmonizing legal frameworks, and providing technical assistance to improve collaboration in criminal matters. Additionally, the development of mutual trust and confidence between countries is vital for successful extradition and effective cooperation in tackling transnational crime.

Future Trends in Criminal Law

The field of criminal law is continuously evolving in response to societal changes, technological advancements, and global challenges. Several future trends are likely to shape the development of criminal law:

1. Advancements in Technology: The increasing use of technology in criminal activities, such as cybercrime, data breaches, and digital currency fraud, will necessitate updates in criminal laws to address these emerging threats effectively.

2. Cybersecurity and Privacy Protections: As cybercrime becomes more prevalent, there will be a growing focus on strengthening cybersecurity laws and protecting individuals' digital privacy rights.

3. Artificial Intelligence and Criminal Justice: The use of artificial intelligence in criminal justice, including predictive policing and risk assessment algorithms, will raise concerns about bias and fairness, leading to the need for guidelines and regulations.

4. Global Cooperation in Criminal Matters: Transnational crime, such as terrorism, human trafficking, and cybercrime, will require enhanced international cooperation and harmonization of laws to combat these offenses effectively.

5. Restorative Justice and Alternative Dispute Resolution: The use of restorative justice practices and alternative dispute resolution mechanisms will continue to grow as a means to address crime and promote reconciliation between victims and offenders.

6. Criminal Justice Reforms: Criminal justice systems in various countries will undergo reforms to address issues like overcriminalization, mass incarceration, and the disproportionate impact of criminal laws on marginalized communities.

7. Addressing White-Collar Crime: Efforts to combat white-collar crime, including corporate fraud and corruption, will gain prominence as these offenses have significant economic and societal implications.

8. Human Rights Protections: Criminal laws will continue to align with international human rights standards to ensure the fair treatment of accused individuals and protect the rights of victims.

9. Rehabilitation and Diversion Programs: There will be increased emphasis on diversion programs and rehabilitation for offenders, particularly for non-violent and low-level offenses, to reduce recidivism and prison overcrowding.

10. Expanding Scope of Criminal Liability: Some jurisdictions may broaden the scope of criminal liability to address new types of offenses, such as environmental crimes, human rights violations, and social media-related offenses.

11. Transparency and Accountability: There will be growing demands for transparency and accountability in law enforcement practices, evidence collection, and use of new technologies in criminal investigations.

12. Community-Based Justice Initiatives: Community-based justice initiatives will gain traction as communities play a more active role in crime prevention and restorative justice processes.

13. Dealing with Transnational Crimes: International efforts to combat transnational crimes will involve cross-border cooperation, intelligence-sharing, and mutual legal assistance agreements.

14. Climate Change and Criminal Law: The impact of

climate change on crime patterns, such as climate-induced migration and environmental degradation, may necessitate new legal responses.

Overall, the future trends in criminal law will revolve around leveraging technology for crime prevention and investigation while safeguarding human rights and promoting innovative approaches to justice and rehabilitation. These trends will shape legal systems' ability to adapt to new challenges and provide effective responses to evolving criminal behaviors and societal needs.

The impact of emerging technologies on crime and law enforcement

Emerging technologies have had a profound impact on crime and law enforcement practices, both positively and negatively. These advancements have presented new opportunities for criminals, while also enabling law enforcement agencies to enhance their investigative capabilities. Here are some key ways emerging technologies have influenced crime and law enforcement:

1. Cybercrime: The digital age has given rise to sophisticated cybercriminal activities, such as hacking, data breaches, ransomware attacks, and identity theft. Criminals exploit vulnerabilities in computer networks and software to commit crimes across borders, making detection and prosecution more challenging for law enforcement.

2. Digital Forensics: Advancements in digital forensics tools and techniques have allowed law enforcement to gather and analyze digital evidence from electronic devices, helping in the investigation of cybercrimes and other offenses involving electronic communications.

3. Surveillance Technologies: Law enforcement agencies now use advanced surveillance technologies, such as facial recognition, drones, and license plate readers, to monitor criminal activities and track suspects. However, concerns about privacy and potential abuses of these technologies have arisen.

4. Predictive Policing: Data analytics and artificial intelligence are used in predictive policing to identify crime patterns and predict where crimes are likely to occur, enabling law enforcement to allocate resources more efficiently.

5. Body-Worn Cameras: The adoption of body-worn cameras by law enforcement officers has increased transparency and accountability during interactions with the public, providing valuable evidence in investigations and reducing allegations of misconduct.

6. Cryptocurrencies: Cryptocurrencies have been used by criminals for money laundering, ransom payments, and illegal transactions, presenting challenges in tracing and recovering illicit funds.

7. Social Media and Online Platforms: Social media platforms and online communication tools have been used for cyberbullying, harassment, spreading extremist ideologies, and organizing criminal activities, posing new challenges for law enforcement to address digital crimes.

8. DNA Technology: Advances in DNA analysis have revolutionized forensic investigations, enabling law enforcement to identify suspects and link individuals to crime scenes more accurately.

9. Artificial Intelligence in Investigations: AI tools can process vast amounts of data to identify patterns and connections, helping law enforcement agencies in solving complex cases.

10. Virtual Currency in Criminal Activities: Virtual currencies like Bitcoin have been used in illicit transactions on the dark web, making it more difficult for law enforcement to trace the flow of money in criminal networks.

11. Data Privacy and Cybersecurity: The proliferation of digital data has heightened concerns about

data privacy and cybersecurity, as criminals exploit weaknesses in information systems to gain unauthorized access to sensitive data.

12. Online Child Exploitation: Emerging technologies have facilitated the spread of child pornography and other forms of child exploitation online, necessitating specialized investigative units and international cooperation to combat these crimes.

Law enforcement agencies must adapt to these technological changes, develop specialized skills, and implement appropriate policies to combat emerging forms of crime effectively. Additionally, balancing the use of advanced technologies with protecting civil liberties and privacy rights is an ongoing challenge for law enforcement and policymakers in the digital age.

The role of artificial intelligence in criminal justice systems

Artificial intelligence (AI) plays a significant role in modern criminal justice systems, influencing various stages of the criminal justice process. AI technologies use algorithms and machine learning to analyze vast amounts of data, make predictions, and support decision-making. Some key roles of AI in criminal justice systems include:

1. Predictive Policing: AI algorithms can analyze historical crime data to identify patterns and trends, helping law enforcement agencies allocate resources more effectively to areas with higher crime rates.

2. Criminal Intelligence Analysis: AI-powered tools can process and analyze large volumes of structured and unstructured data to generate actionable intelligence for law enforcement agencies, aiding in the investigation of criminal activities.

3. Facial Recognition: AI-based facial recognition systems assist in identifying suspects by comparing images captured from surveillance cameras or other sources with databases of known individuals.

4. Automated Case Management: AI technologies can streamline case management processes, assisting law enforcement in organizing and prioritizing cases, managing evidence, and tracking case progress.

5. Sentencing and Risk Assessment: AI algorithms can be used to assess the risk of recidivism and inform sentencing decisions, though concerns about bias and

fairness must be addressed.

6. Evidence Analysis: AI tools can assist in analyzing digital evidence, such as data retrieved from computers, mobile devices, and social media, supporting investigations and court proceedings.

7. Language Processing and Translation: AI can aid in processing and translating multilingual documents, which is particularly useful in international criminal investigations.

8. Virtual Legal Assistants: AI-powered virtual assistants can provide legal information and answer basic questions for individuals seeking legal guidance.

9. Forensic Analysis: AI applications can enhance forensic analysis, including fingerprint and DNA matching, and automate tedious tasks in crime scene investigation.

10. Courtroom Decision Support: AI technologies can provide judges and attorneys with relevant case law, legal precedents, and research, aiding in informed decision-making.

11. Criminal Profiling: AI can help in creating criminal profiles by analyzing crime scene characteristics, behavioral patterns, and historical data.

12. Parole and Probation Management: AI-based systems can assess the risk of parolees and probationers violating their terms, aiding in personalized supervision and interventions.

While AI offers numerous advantages in criminal justice, there are also challenges and concerns. Ensuring the fairness, transparency, and accountability of AI algorithms is critical to avoid bias and discrimination. Striking a balance between efficiency and protecting civil liberties, privacy, and due process rights is an ongoing challenge. Additionally, the use of AI in the criminal justice system requires appropriate training for law enforcement personnel and legal professionals to understand AI outputs and use them responsibly.

Innovations in criminal law and policy-making

Innovations in criminal law and policy-making are crucial for addressing emerging challenges, improving the effectiveness of justice systems, and upholding human rights. Several key innovations have been introduced in recent years to enhance criminal law and policy:

1. Restorative Justice Programs: Restorative justice focuses on repairing harm caused by crimes through dialogue, reconciliation, and restitution. These programs prioritize the needs of victims and aim to reintegrate offenders into the community.

2. Diversion Programs: Diversion programs offer alternatives to traditional prosecution, particularly for non-violent offenders. They may involve counseling, education, or community service, aiming to reduce recidivism and lessen the burden on the criminal justice system.

3. Drug Courts and Mental Health Courts: Specialized courts focus on addressing substance abuse and mental health issues that often underlie criminal behavior. These courts provide treatment and support rather than incarceration.

4. Sentencing Reforms: Many jurisdictions are reevaluating sentencing practices, moving away from mandatory minimums and implementing evidence-based sentencing models that consider factors such as the offender's risk level and rehabilitation prospects.

5. Expungement and Record Sealing: Policies allowing individuals with non-violent criminal records to seal or expunge their records after a certain period have been enacted to facilitate reintegration into society and improve employment prospects.

6. Data-Driven Policy Making: Governments and policymakers are increasingly using data analytics and evidence-based research to inform criminal justice policy decisions, improving the overall efficiency and effectiveness of interventions.

7. Transparency and Accountability Initiatives: Efforts to increase transparency and accountability in law enforcement include the use of body-worn cameras, citizen oversight boards, and enhanced data reporting on use-of-force incidents.

8. Alternatives to Incarceration: Policies promoting alternatives to incarceration, such as community service, electronic monitoring, and supervised release, aim to reduce prison populations and promote rehabilitation.

9. Decriminalization of Certain Offenses: Some jurisdictions have decriminalized or reduced penalties for certain offenses, such as possession of small amounts of marijuana, to focus on more serious crimes.

10. International Cooperation on Cross-Border Crime: Global challenges like cybercrime, human trafficking, and terrorism require international cooperation and harmonized policies to combat transnational crime effectively.

11. Community Engagement and Policing Reforms: Policymakers are emphasizing community engagement and collaboration to foster trust between law enforcement and the communities they serve.

12. Human Rights-Based Approaches: Criminal justice policies are increasingly adopting human rights-based

frameworks, ensuring respect for the rights of accused individuals, victims, and vulnerable populations.

13. Legal Aid and Access to Justice: Policies aimed at enhancing access to legal representation and support services for marginalized populations help promote fairness and equal treatment in the justice system.

14. Technology Integration: The integration of technology in criminal law and policy-making includes using AI for predictive policing, digital evidence analysis, and online dispute resolution.

Innovations in criminal law and policy continue to evolve in response to societal needs, technological advancements, and a growing recognition of the importance of fairness, accountability, and rehabilitation in the criminal justice system. Policymakers, legal professionals, and stakeholders must continue to collaborate and adapt to ensure a just and effective criminal justice system.

Recapitulation of key insights and themes discussed in the book

"Justice in Motion: Exploring the Dynamics of Criminal Law" delves into various aspects of criminal law and its evolving role in contemporary society. Throughout the book, key insights and themes emerge, contributing to a comprehensive understanding of the subject:

1. Criminal Law's Significance: The book emphasizes the critical role of criminal law in maintaining social order, protecting individual rights, and promoting justice within a society.
2. Historical Development: Readers gain insights into the historical evolution of criminal law, from ancient systems of justice to modern legal frameworks.
3. Foundational Principles: Core principles such as the presumption of innocence, burden of proof, actus reus, and mens rea are explored, highlighting the importance of fairness and accountability in criminal proceedings.
4. Technology's Impact: The book extensively covers the influence of emerging technologies on crime and law enforcement, with discussions on cybercrime, digital evidence, AI, and its implications for privacy and civil liberties.
5. Human Rights in Criminal Justice: The protection of human rights, prohibition of torture, fair trial rights, and access to legal representation are recurring themes, emphasizing the importance of upholding

rights in criminal proceedings.

6. Alternatives to Traditional Justice: Innovations like restorative justice, diversion programs, and problem-solving courts offer promising alternatives to traditional punitive approaches.

7. Global Perspectives: The book delves into international cooperation, transnational crime, and comparative analysis of criminal justice systems, highlighting the need for global collaboration in addressing crime.

8. Criminal Law Reforms: Various chapters explore reforms aimed at reducing recidivism, addressing systemic biases, and enhancing transparency and accountability in the criminal justice system.

9. Social Justice and Vulnerable Populations: The book emphasizes the importance of addressing social injustices, protecting vulnerable populations, and promoting equality in criminal law.

10. Balancing Technology and Privacy: A recurring theme is the need to strike a balance between using technology for crime prevention and respecting privacy rights and civil liberties.

11. Restorative Justice: The potential of restorative justice in repairing harm, fostering reconciliation, and promoting rehabilitation is explored, offering an alternative approach to punitive justice.

12. Access to Justice: The book highlights the importance of ensuring access to legal representation and legal aid for all individuals, particularly those from marginalized communities.

13. Data-Driven Policy Making: Evidence-based research and data analytics are seen as essential tools in formulating effective criminal justice policies and interventions.

14. Future Directions: The book looks ahead to the future of criminal law, discussing how innovations, technological advancements, and global challenges

will shape criminal justice systems.

Overall, "Justice in Motion: Exploring the Dynamics of Criminal Law" provides readers with a comprehensive overview of criminal law's multifaceted nature and its significance in a rapidly changing world. The insights gained from this exploration highlight the complexities, opportunities, and challenges that underpin criminal justice systems worldwide.

A call to action for promoting a more just and effective criminal justice system

As we navigate the complexities of the criminal justice system, it is crucial to recognize the imperative for promoting a more just and effective system that upholds the principles of fairness, equality, and human rights. To achieve this transformative vision, a resolute call to action is necessary:

1. Embrace Restorative Justice: Emphasize the adoption of restorative justice principles, promoting dialogue, reconciliation, and accountability between offenders, victims, and communities. Invest in restorative justice programs that prioritize healing and rehabilitation over punitive measures.

2. Address Systemic Biases: Confront and dismantle systemic biases that perpetuate inequality within the criminal justice system. Implement policies that eliminate racial and socioeconomic disparities and ensure equitable treatment for all individuals.

3. Strengthen Legal Representation: Advocate for increased access to legal representation and legal aid for marginalized and vulnerable populations, ensuring that everyone receives fair and competent representation regardless of their socio-economic status.

4. Promote Alternatives to Incarceration: Champion diversion programs, problem-solving courts, and community-based sentencing as alternatives to traditional incarceration. Prioritize rehabilitation and

reintegration efforts to reduce recidivism rates.

5. Enhance Police Accountability: Support efforts to improve transparency, oversight, and accountability within law enforcement agencies. Advocate for the use of body-worn cameras, citizen review boards, and clear policies on the use of force.

6. Embrace Evidence-Based Policy Making: Advocate for data-driven policy making that relies on evidence, research, and expert analysis to shape effective criminal justice reforms. Prioritize evidence-based programs that have proven to be successful in reducing crime and promoting rehabilitation.

7. Address Technology and Privacy Concerns: Encourage the development of technology that enhances crime prevention and investigation while safeguarding privacy rights and civil liberties. Advocate for clear guidelines on the use of surveillance technologies and data protection measures.

8. Foster Collaboration and International Cooperation: Promote global collaboration and sharing of best practices to combat transnational crime effectively. Advocate for mutual legal assistance agreements and international standards that uphold human rights in criminal justice proceedings.

9. Invest in Rehabilitation and Reintegration: Advocate for comprehensive support systems that address the root causes of criminal behavior and provide opportunities for education, job training, and mental health services to facilitate successful reintegration into society.

10. Educate and Engage: Foster public awareness and education on criminal justice issues. Engage with communities, policymakers, and stakeholders to build support for progressive reforms that prioritize justice, compassion, and equity.

11. Support Victims' Rights: Advocate for comprehensive

support services for victims of crime, ensuring their voices are heard and their rights are protected throughout the criminal justice process.

12. Promote Smart Sentencing: Push for sentencing reforms that focus on the proportionality of punishments, taking into account individual circumstances and rehabilitation prospects.

In conclusion, this call to action seeks to inspire collective efforts to transform our criminal justice system into one that exemplifies justice, compassion, and effectiveness. By advocating for restorative practices, addressing biases, prioritizing rehabilitation, embracing technology responsibly, and fostering global cooperation, we can create a criminal justice system that truly serves the needs of all members of society. Together, we can build a more just and effective criminal justice system that values human dignity, promotes rehabilitation, and upholds the principles of fairness and equality for all.

The importance of ongoing dialogue and research in shaping the future of criminal law

Ongoing dialogue and research are essential for shaping the future of criminal law in a rapidly changing world. The importance of these aspects cannot be overstated, as they offer numerous benefits and opportunities:

1. Addressing Evolving Challenges: Criminal law needs to adapt to emerging challenges such as cybercrime, technology-enabled offenses, and transnational criminal activities. Ongoing dialogue and research enable policymakers and legal experts to understand these challenges better and devise effective responses.

2. Enhancing Evidence-Based Policymaking: Sound research provides empirical evidence and data to inform criminal law policymaking. Evidence-based approaches ensure that laws and policies are grounded in research findings and have a higher likelihood of achieving their intended outcomes.

3. Promoting Reforms and Innovation: Dialogue among legal professionals, academics, activists, and policymakers fosters a culture of innovation. Open discussions and research findings can lead to the identification of areas in need of reform and the development of novel, progressive solutions.

4. Ensuring Human Rights Protection: Criminal law has a direct impact on the rights of individuals, both accused and victims. Ongoing dialogue and research contribute to creating legal frameworks that respect

and protect human rights throughout the criminal justice process.

5. Addressing Systemic Biases: Honest conversations and research can shed light on systemic biases and disparities within the criminal justice system. Understanding these issues is vital for implementing reforms that promote fairness, equality, and justice.

6. Building Public Awareness and Engagement: Engaging the public in ongoing dialogue about criminal law and its impact fosters informed citizenship. Public awareness can lead to greater support for reforms and policies that prioritize justice and rehabilitation over punitive measures.

7. Fostering Collaboration and International Standards: Ongoing dialogue and research facilitate collaboration among different jurisdictions and countries. By sharing knowledge and experiences, nations can work together to develop international standards that uphold human rights and combat transnational crime effectively.

8. Promoting Accountability and Transparency: Continuous dialogue helps in holding institutions accountable for their actions and decision-making processes. Transparency in research and discussions ensures that the public can assess the fairness and effectiveness of the criminal justice system.

9. Supporting Evidence-Based Criminal Justice Interventions: Researchers and experts can evaluate the effectiveness of criminal justice programs and interventions. Their findings can support evidence-based practices that lead to better outcomes in crime prevention and rehabilitation.

10. Encouraging Continuous Improvement: Criminal law is an evolving field that requires ongoing evaluation and improvement. Dialogue and research provide a mechanism for continuous learning and refinement of

legal systems and practices.

In conclusion, ongoing dialogue and research play a pivotal role in shaping the future of criminal law by promoting evidence-based policymaking, addressing emerging challenges, upholding human rights, and fostering innovation. Through collaboration, transparency, and public engagement, societies can build a criminal justice system that reflects the values of justice, fairness, and compassion, while effectively addressing the complexities of crime and the changing landscape of the modern world.

www.ingramcontent.com/pod-product-compliance
Lightning Source LLC
Chambersburg PA
CBHW072207290526
45794CB00004B/1684